MASKS

Colouring Book
Inspired in Rapa Nui & Maori Art

Illustrated by
Jorge Lulić

All Rights Reserved. Copyright © Jorge Lulić 2018
Disclaimer
No part of this book may be reproduced or transmitted in any form or by any means, mechanical or electronic including photocopying or recording, or by an information storage and retrieval system or transmitted by e-mail without permission in writing from the publisher.

Published by Jorge Lulić Fine Art and Print Publications Alicante, Spain.
The book author retains sole copyright to the design and artwork in this book.
jorgelulic556@gmail.com
www.jorgelulic.com

RAPA NUI

Rapa Nui, or Easter Island, as it was to become known, is a beautiful Chilean island situated in Polynesia, in the South East Pacific Ocean, 3,700km (2,300 miles) off the west coast of Chile.

One of the most mystifying and mysterious places on earth, Easter Island is famous for the large monumental Moai statues, which adorn the island.

Easter Island is also home to extensive rock art carvings, called petroglyphs, with unique designs and motifs - in particular the 'Birdman' with its huge eye and bird beak.

MAORI

Maori are the indigenous people of Aotearoa - New Zealand.

New Zealand is a country located in the south west of the Pacific Ocean, about 2000km south east of Australia, in the Tasman Sea.

Art has been an integral element of Maori culture. The colours red, black and white are a strong feature in Maori art.

Traditional arts of the Maori people include carving in wood, stone, or bone, geometrical designs in plaiting and weaving, painted designs on wood and on tattooing.

Colouring tips:

- When it comes to colouring, think about using all of the space you have to fill with whichever colours you like the most. You can experiment by shading and colouring different backgrounds.

- Use either pencils or markers and always test your markers or pencils before your start colouring.

- Remember the ink from markers might bleed through the page, or the inks might run, so place another piece of paper behind the page you're colouring to protect the page behind.

- Pencils will allow you to blend colours, and are very good for fine details. If you like using pencils, buy the biggest selection of colours you can, and keep them well sharpened.

- Lastly: Study the picture carefully before you start, slow down, take your time, and enjoy the process of colouring, and watch your artwork come to life!

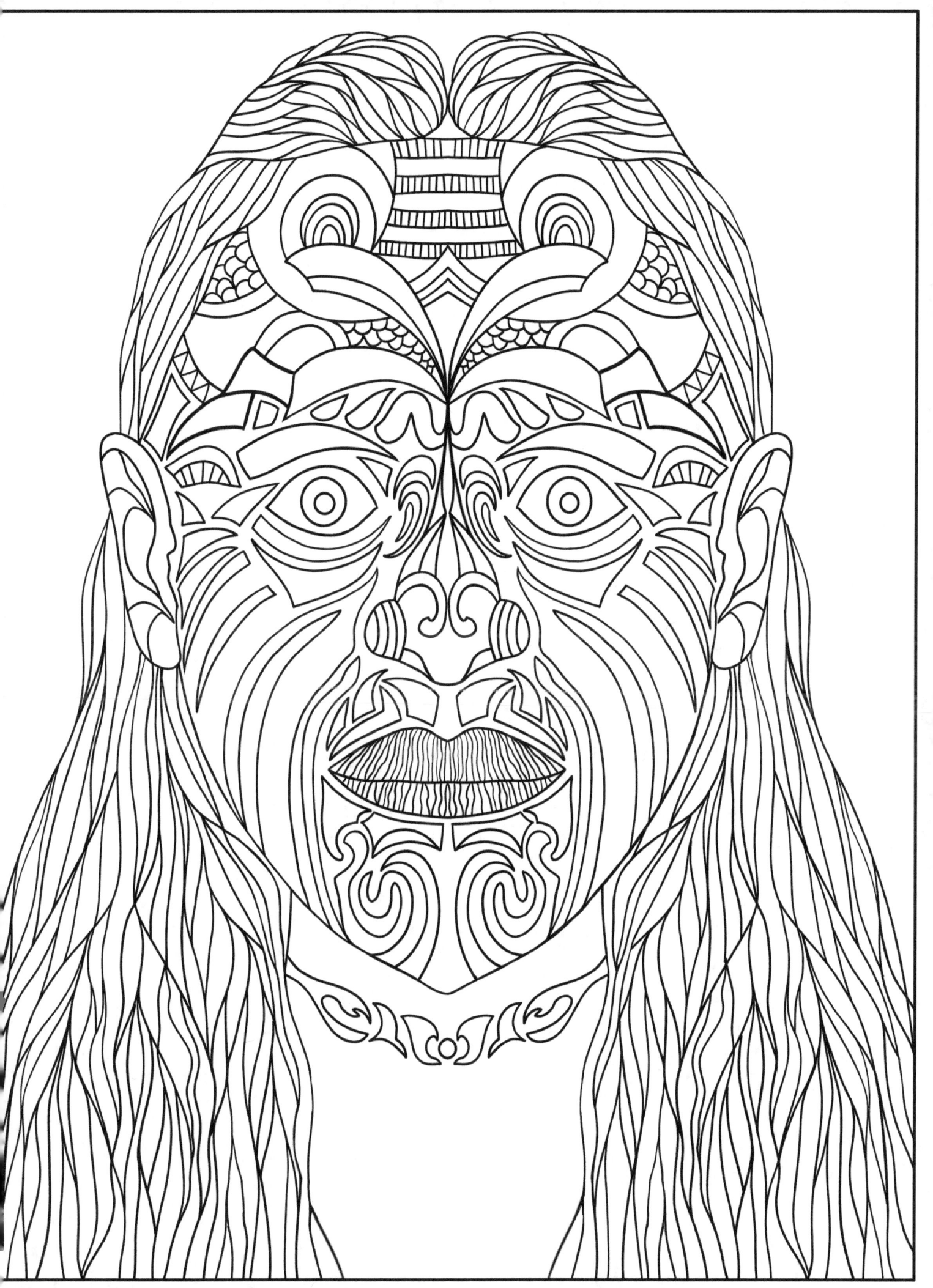

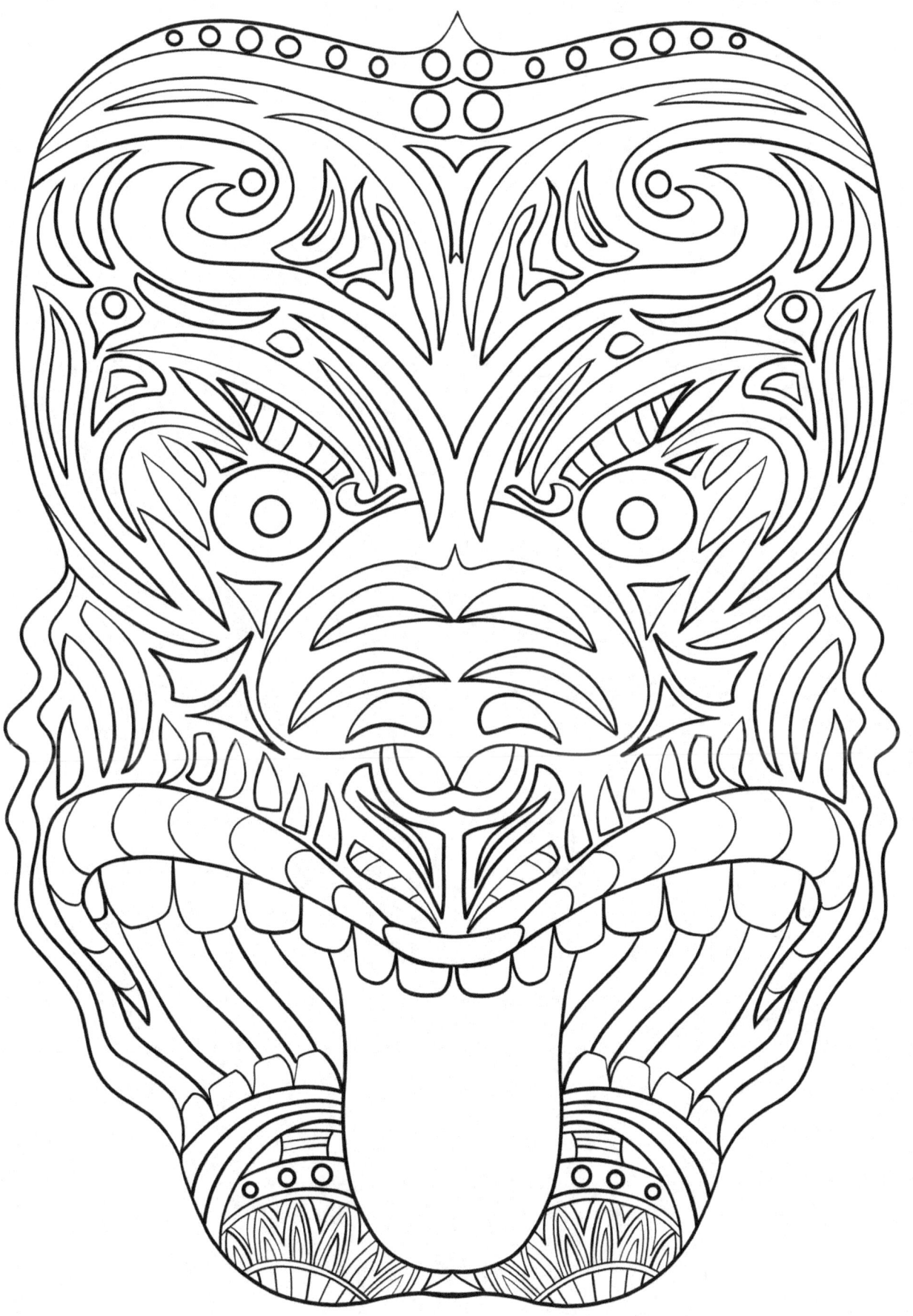

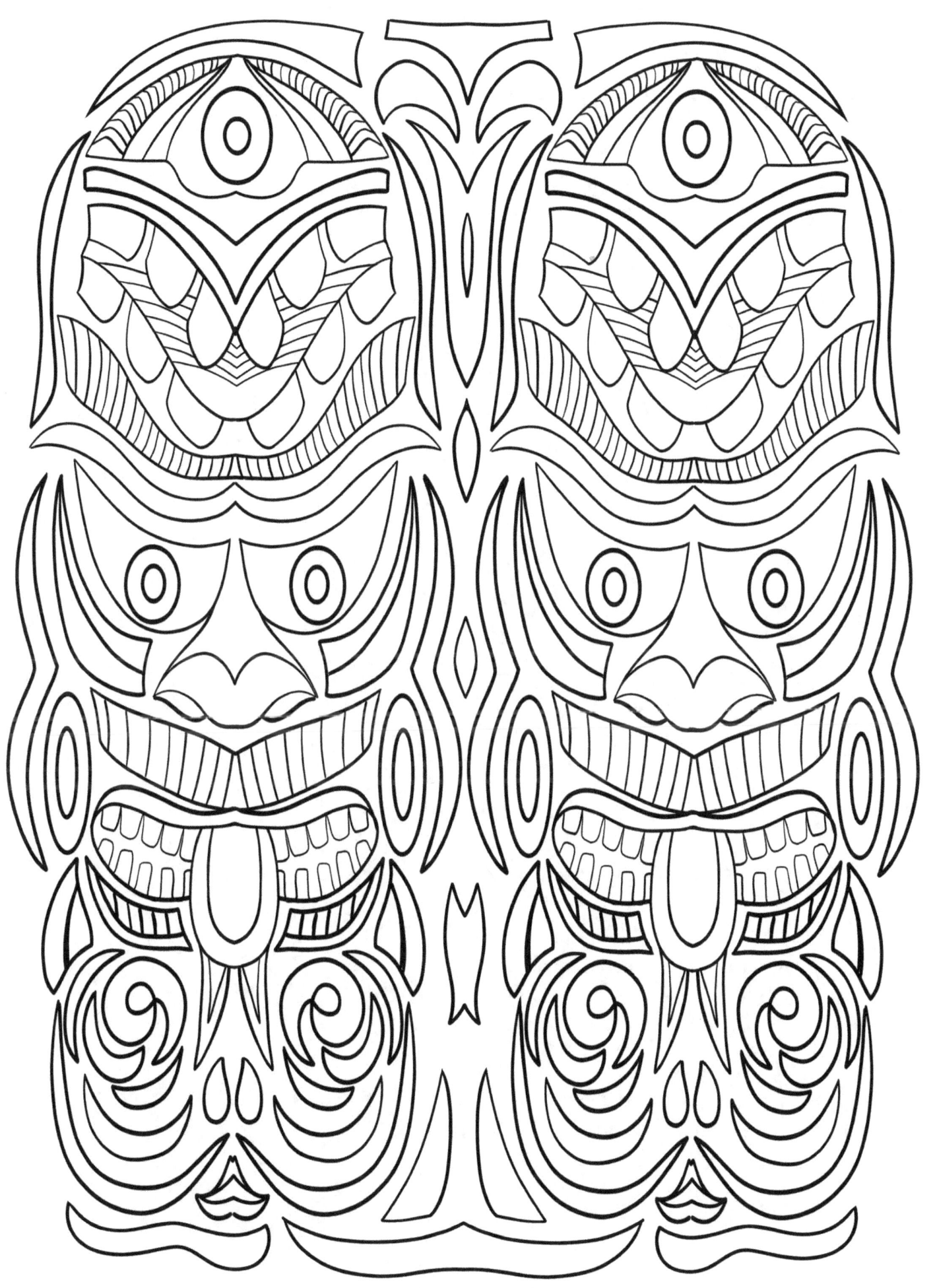

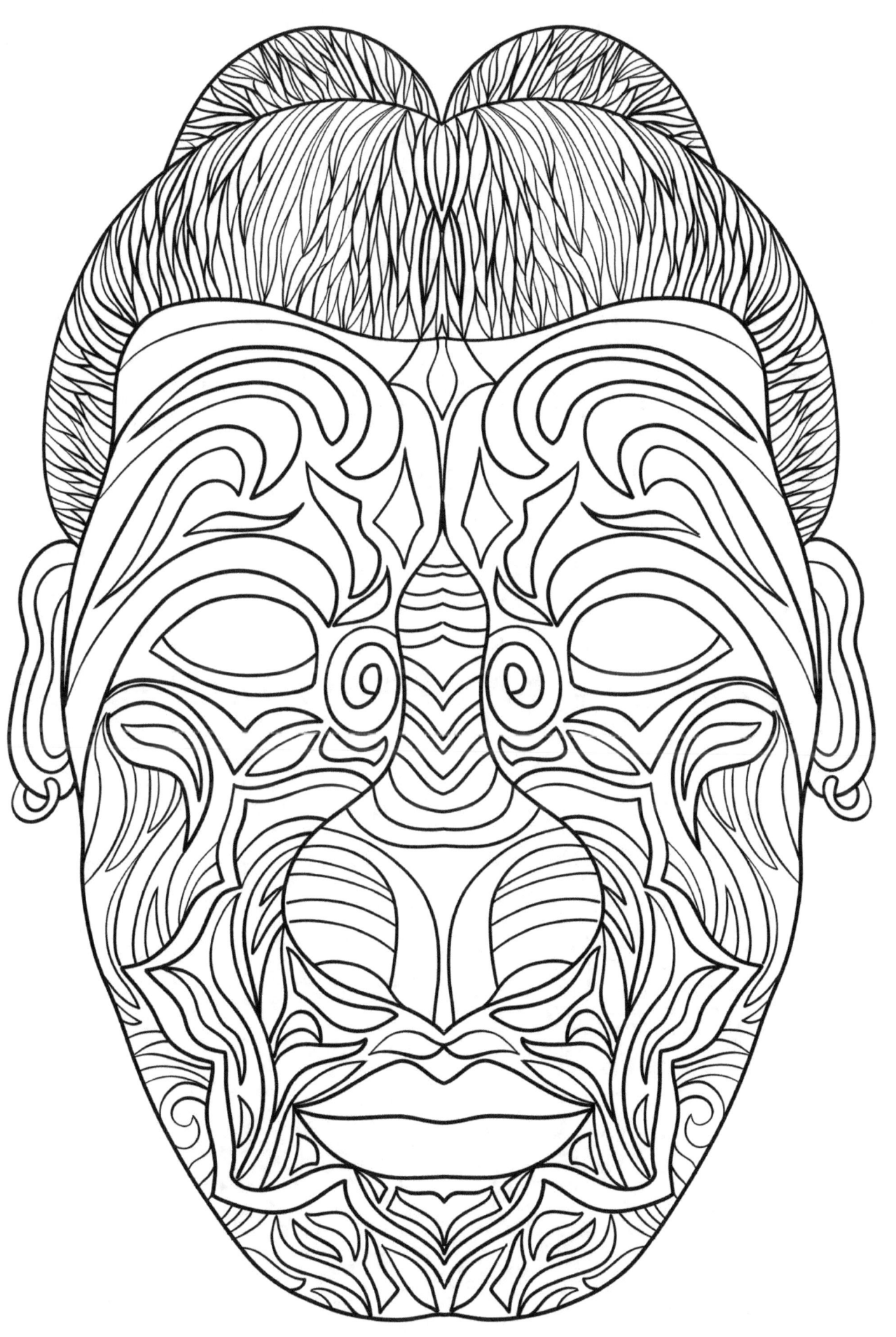

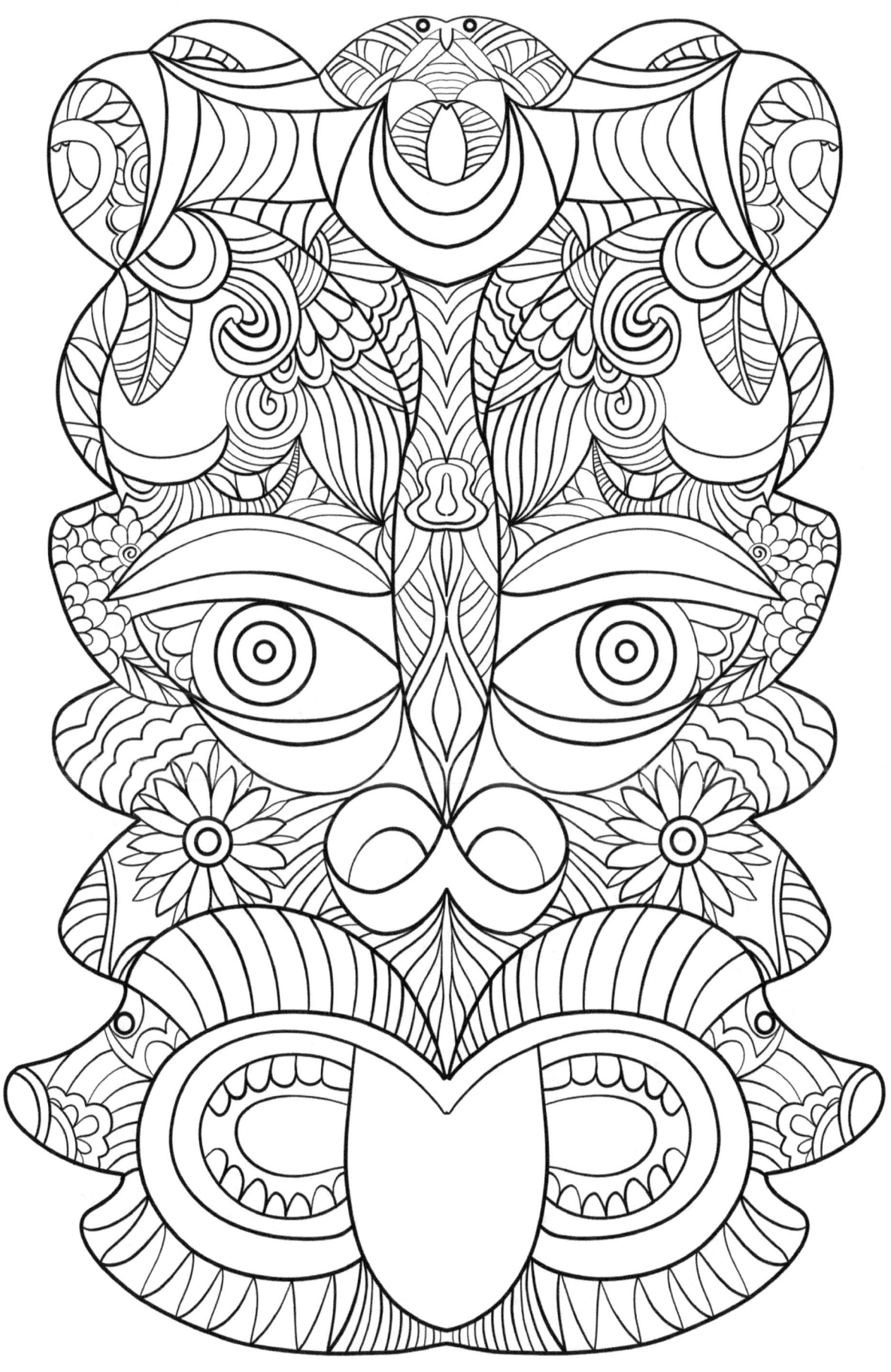

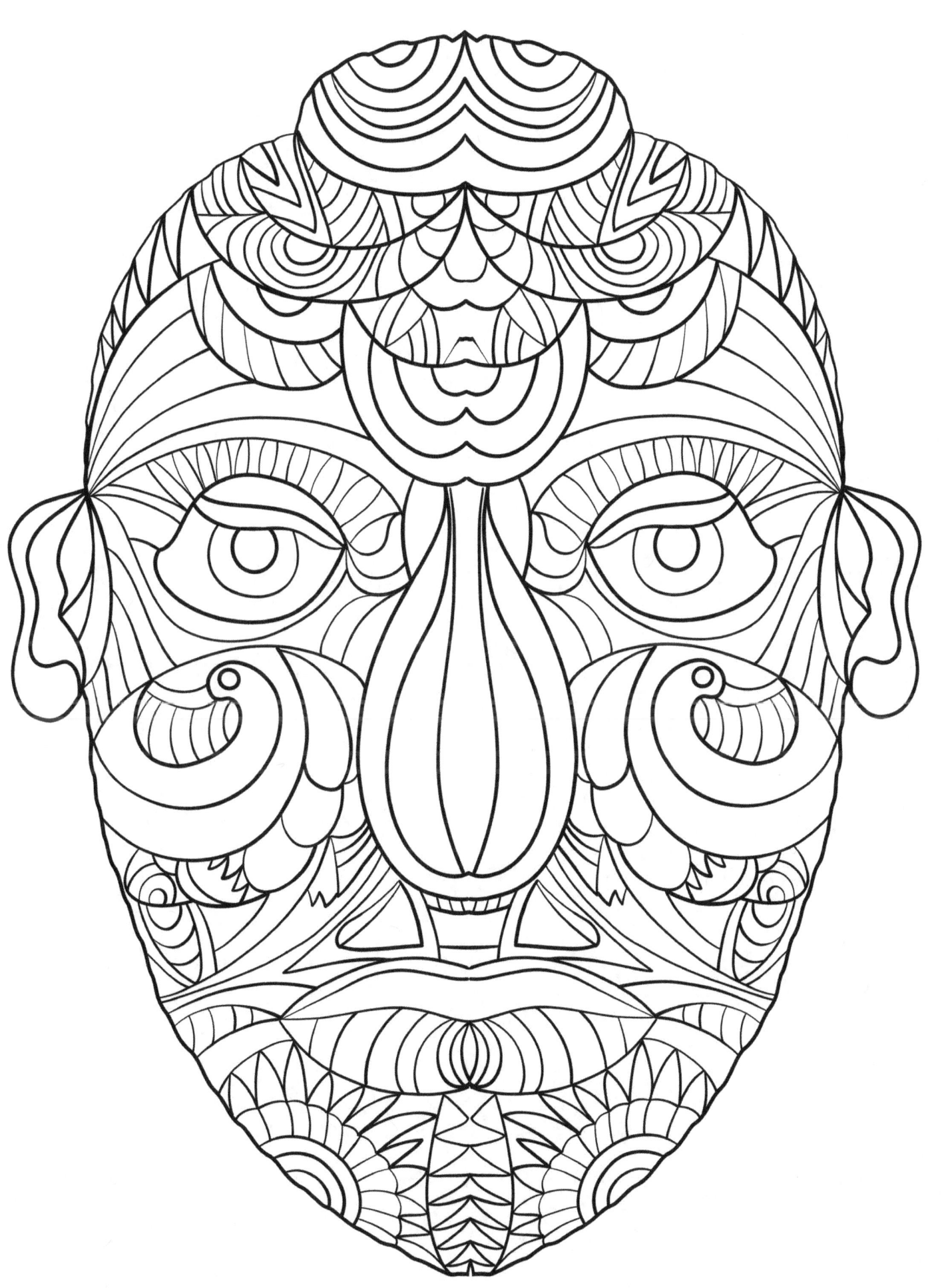

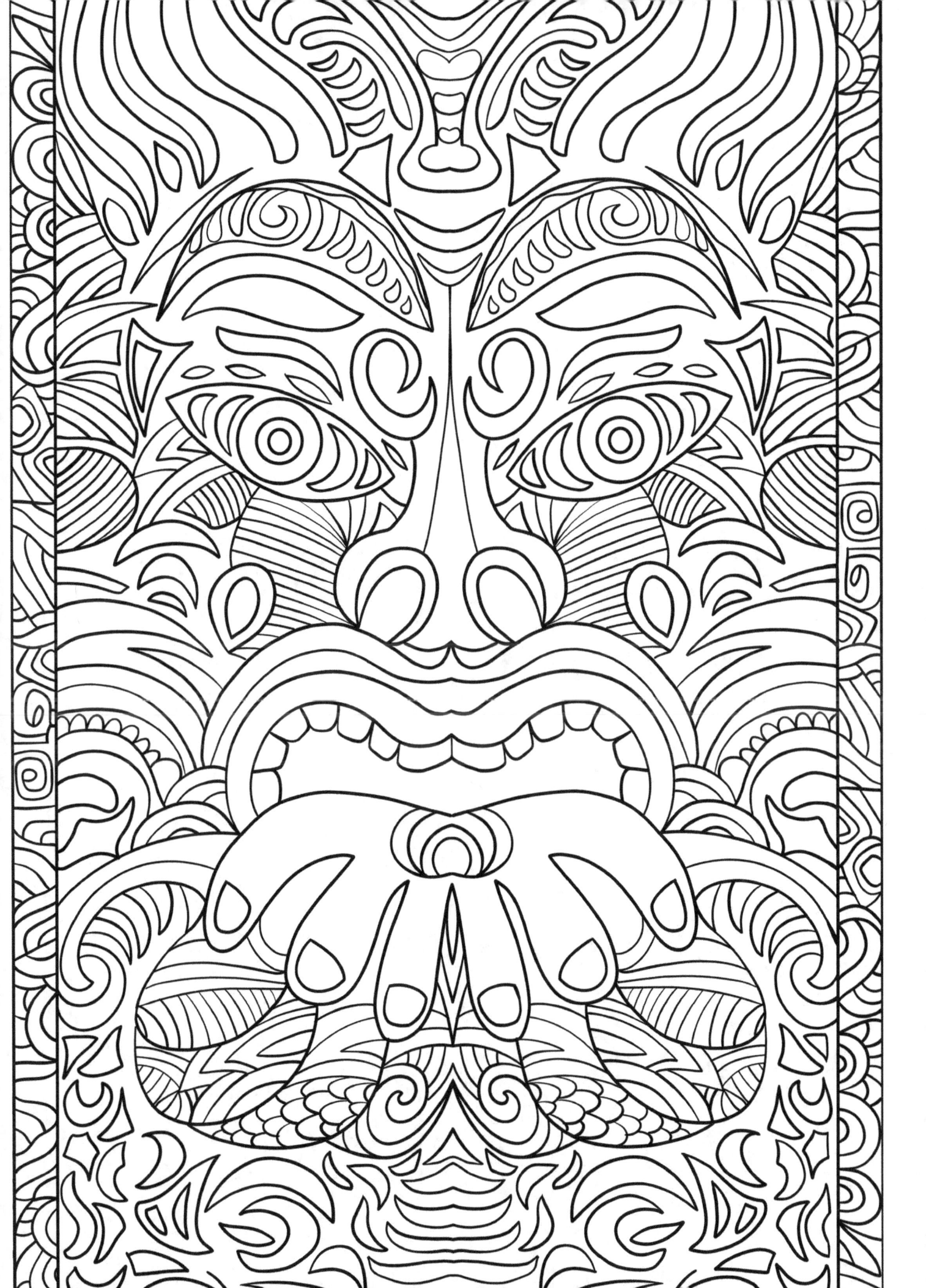

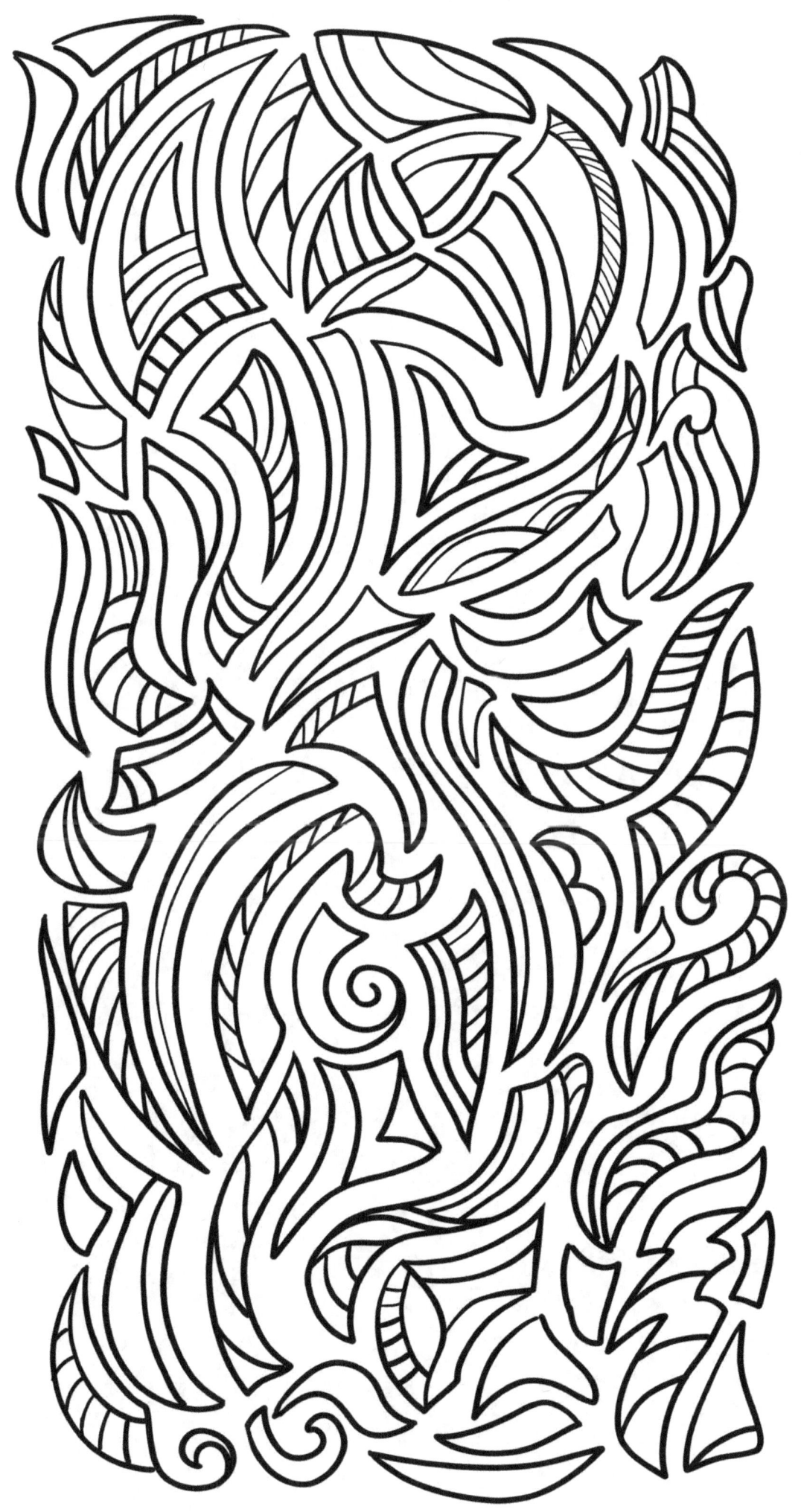

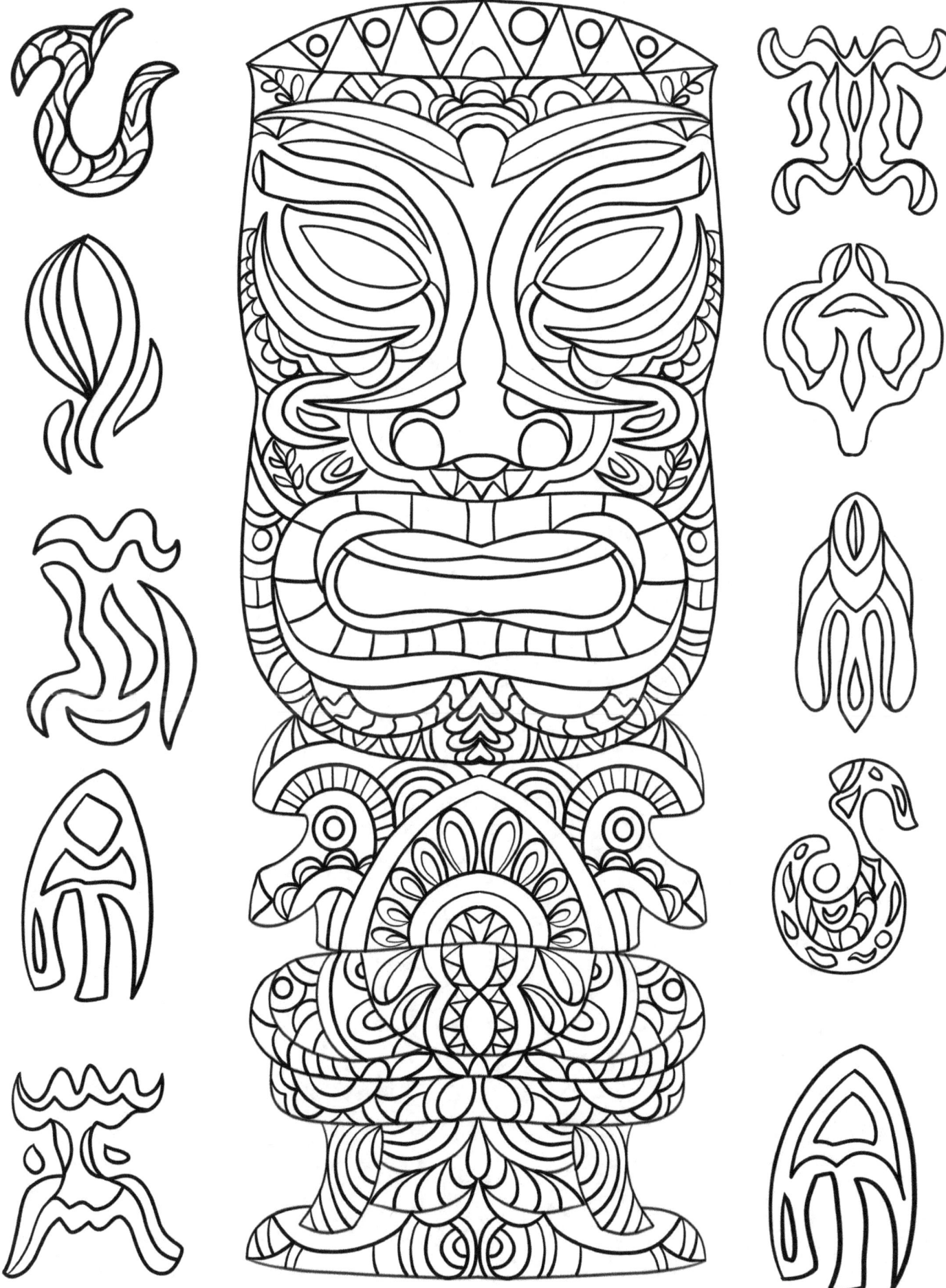

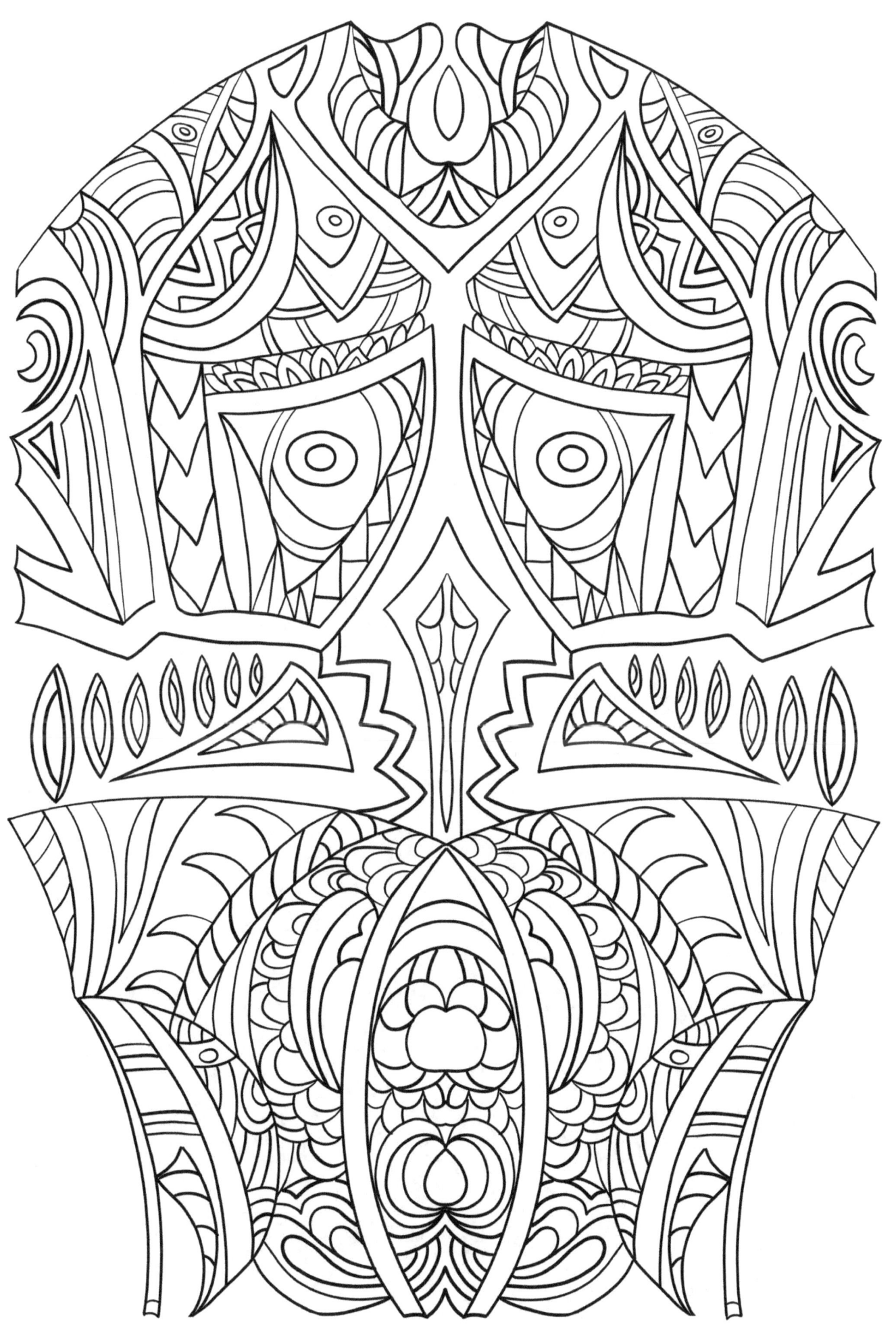

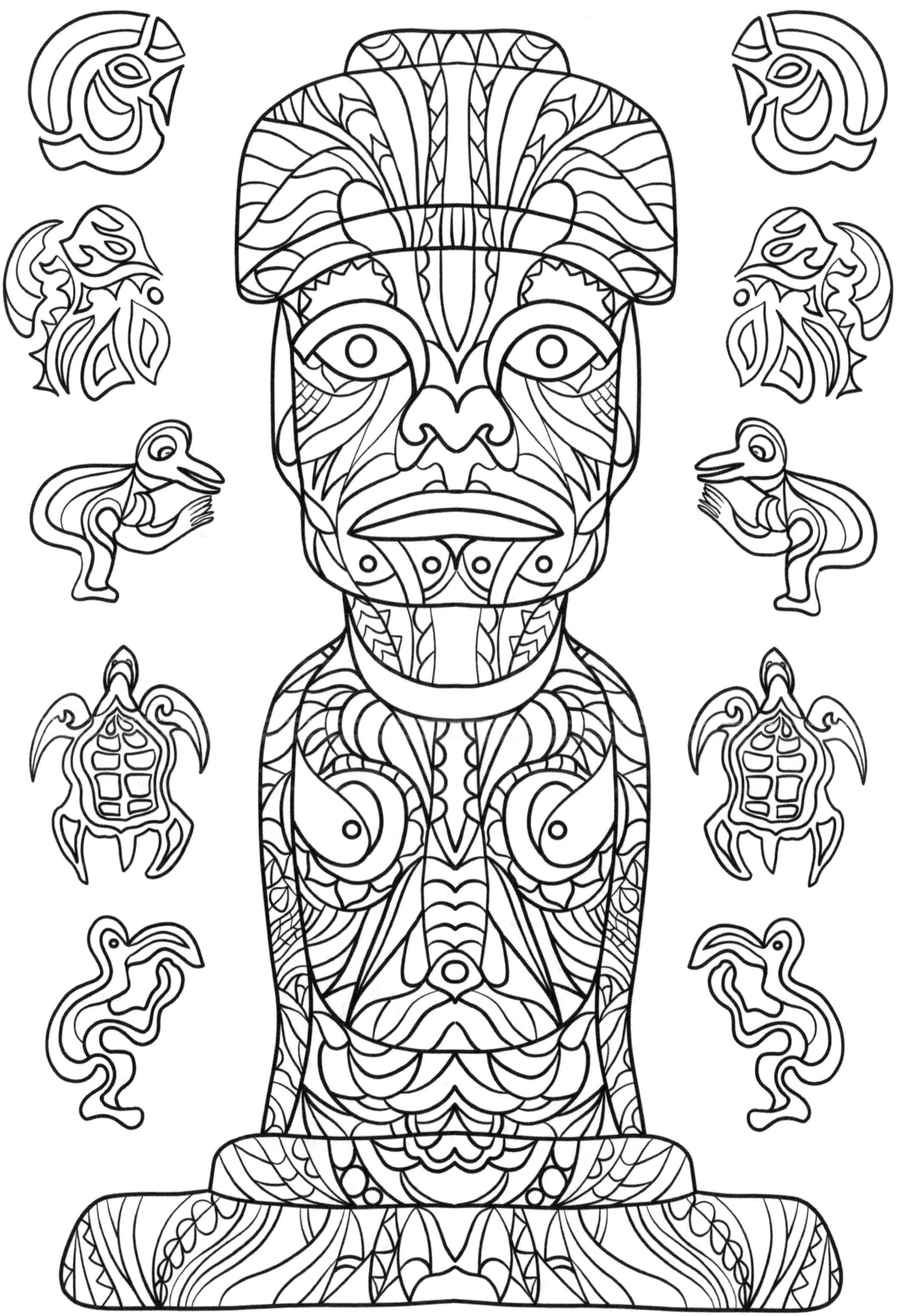

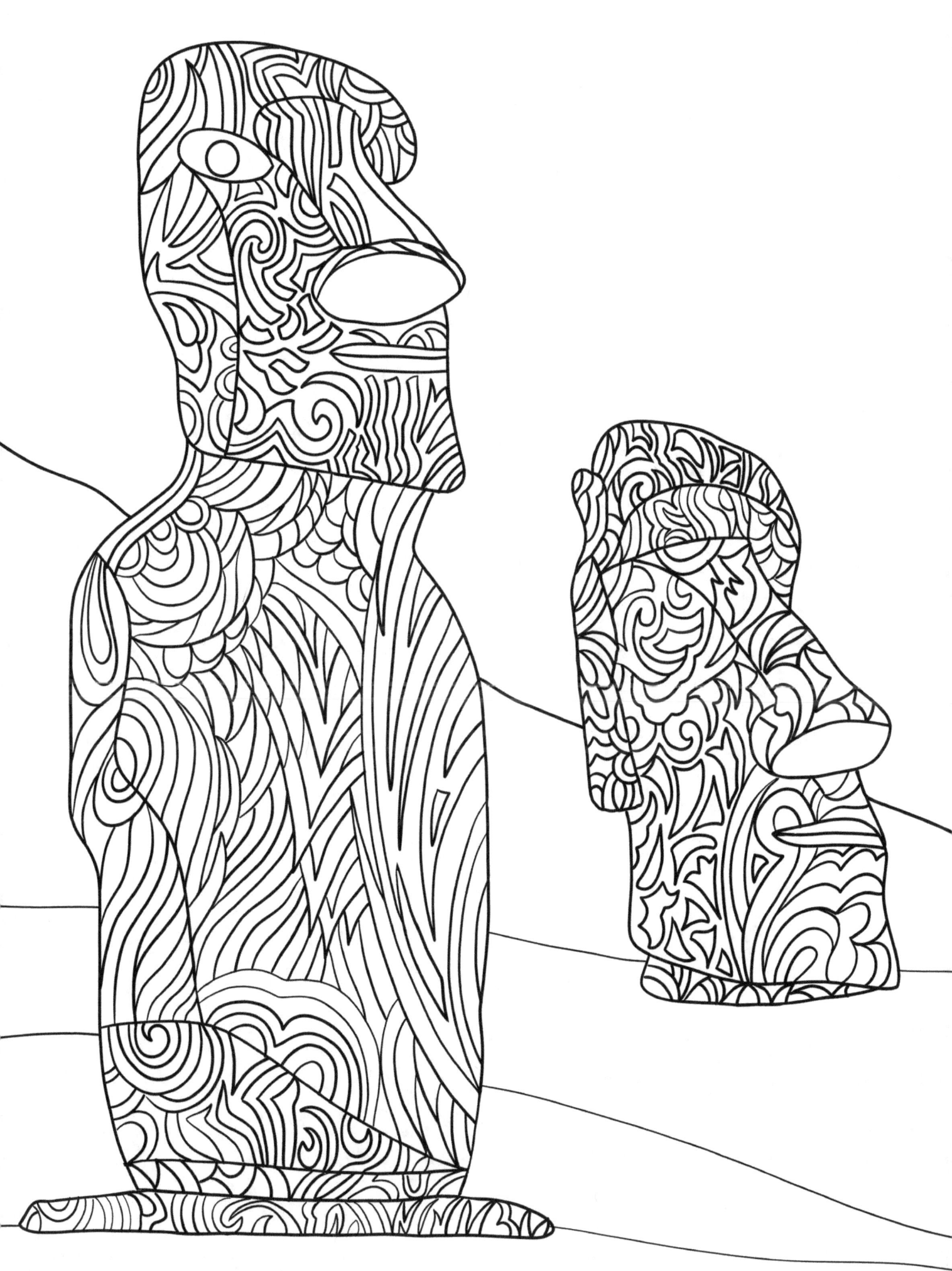

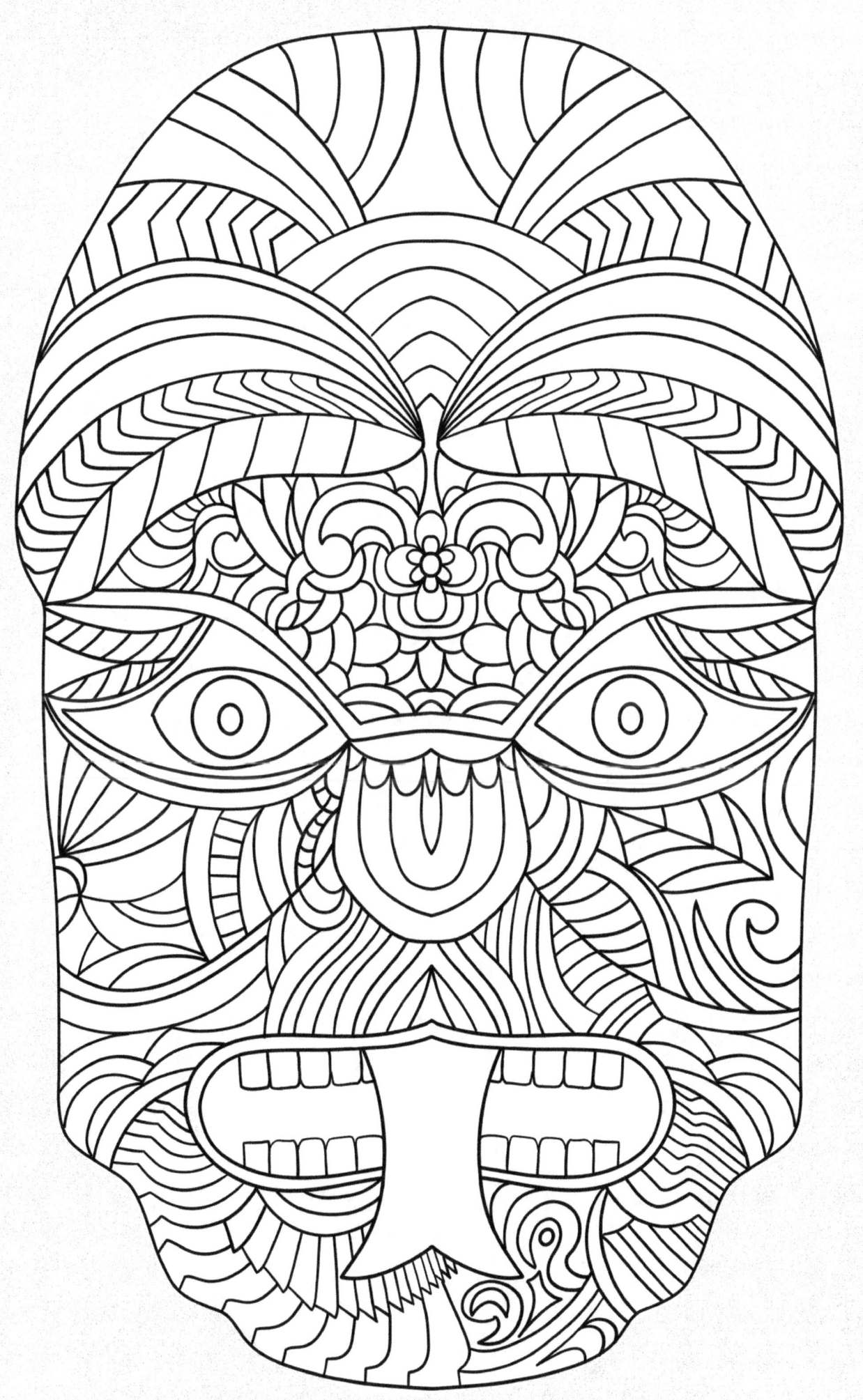

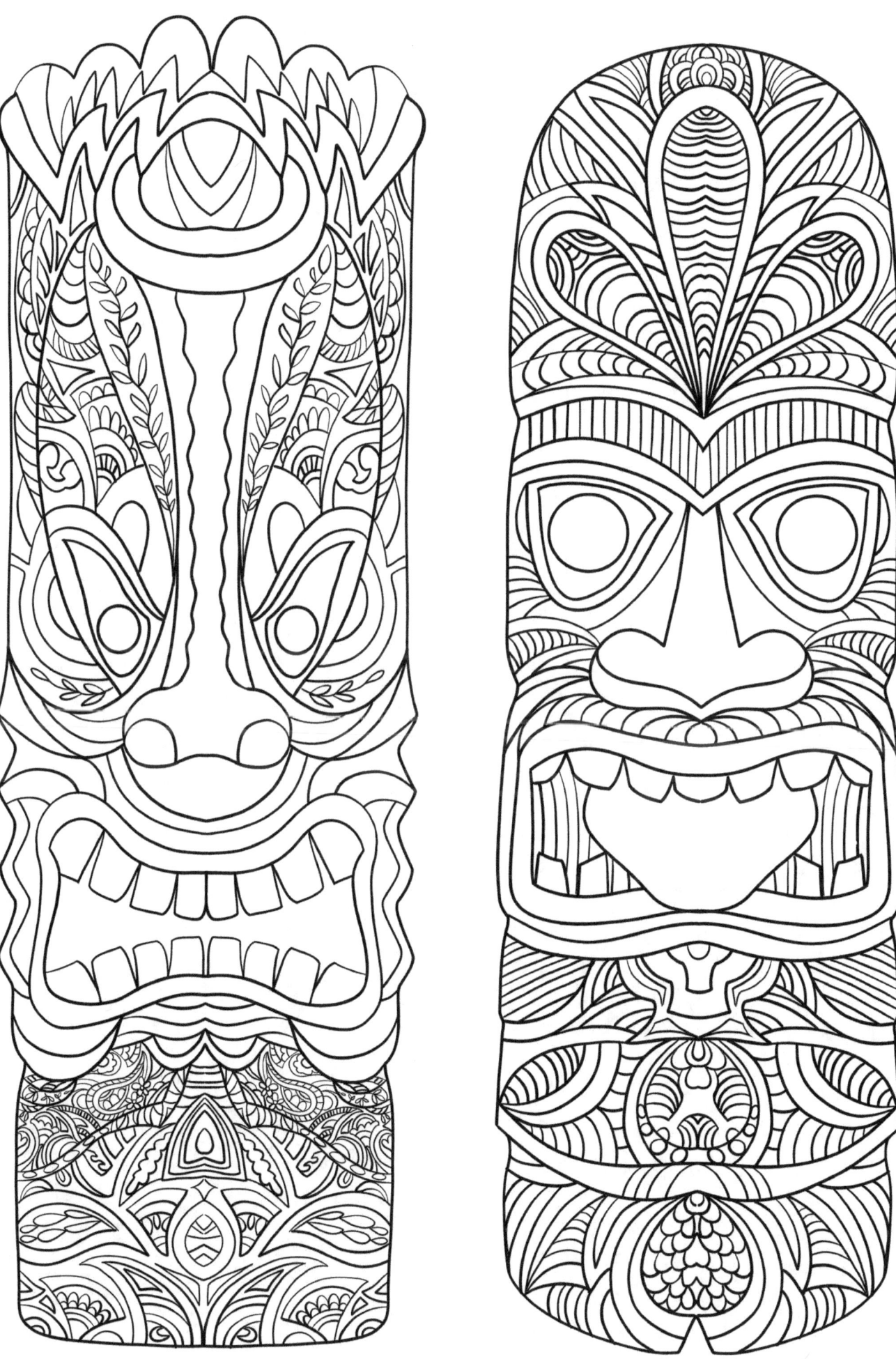

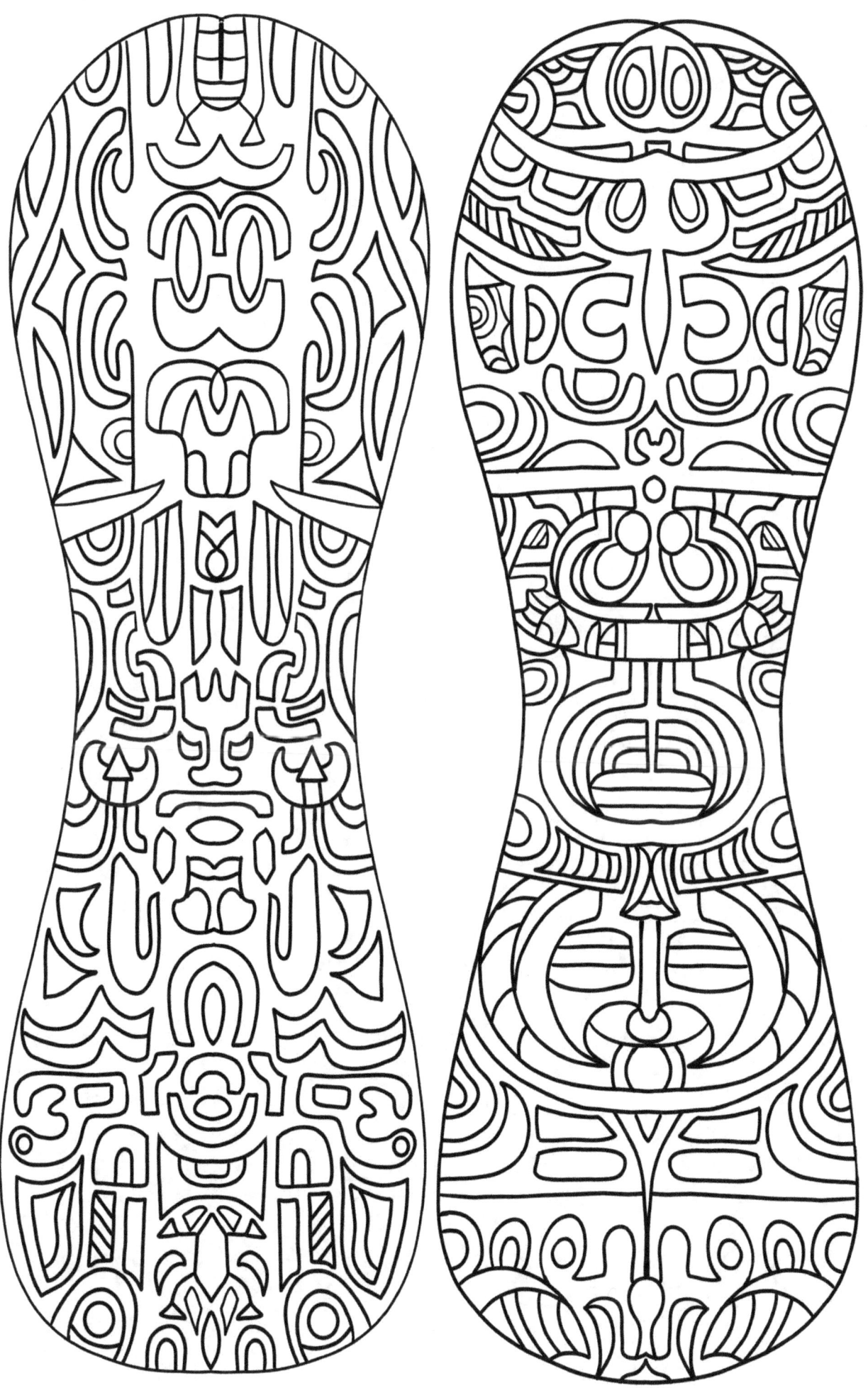

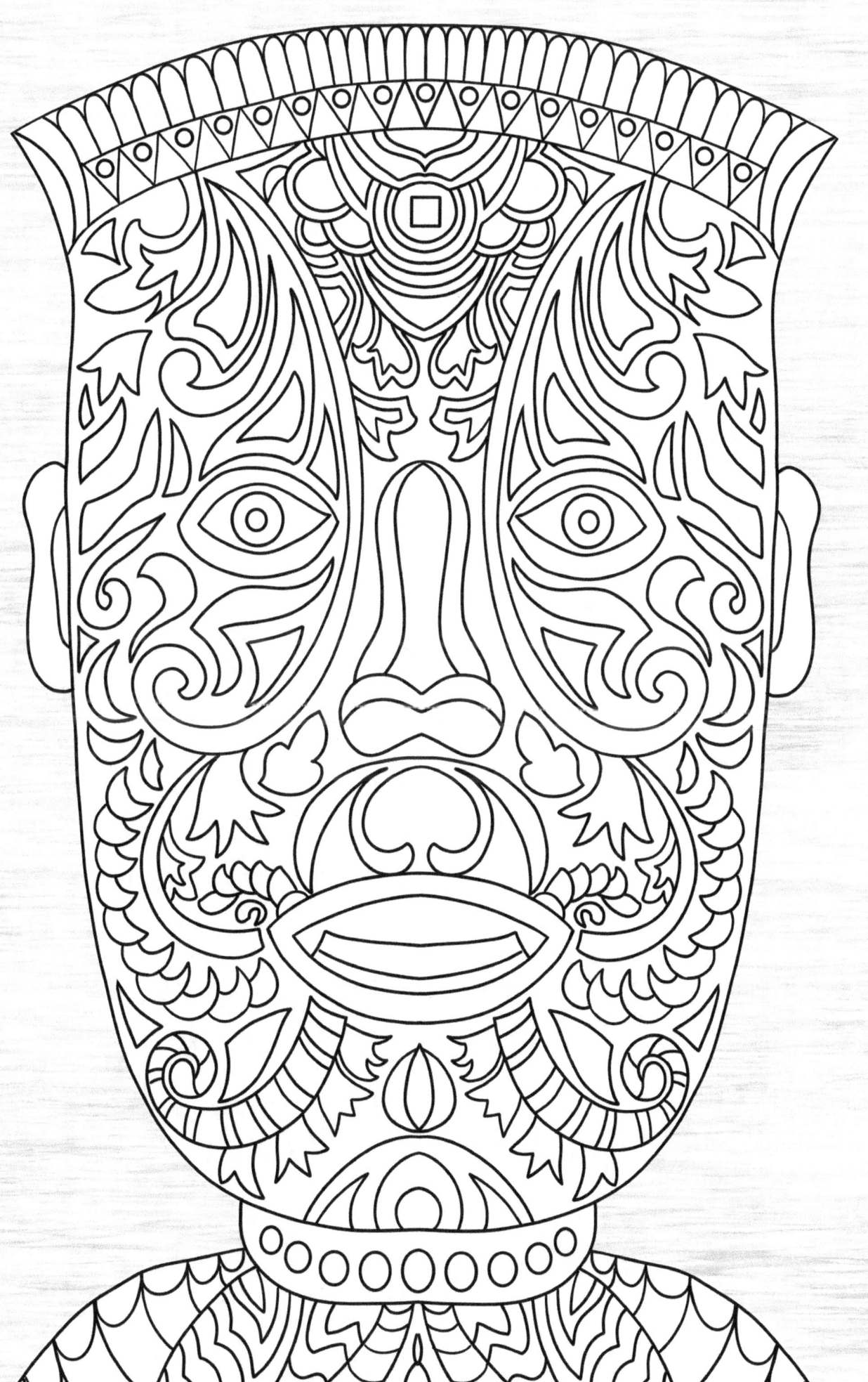

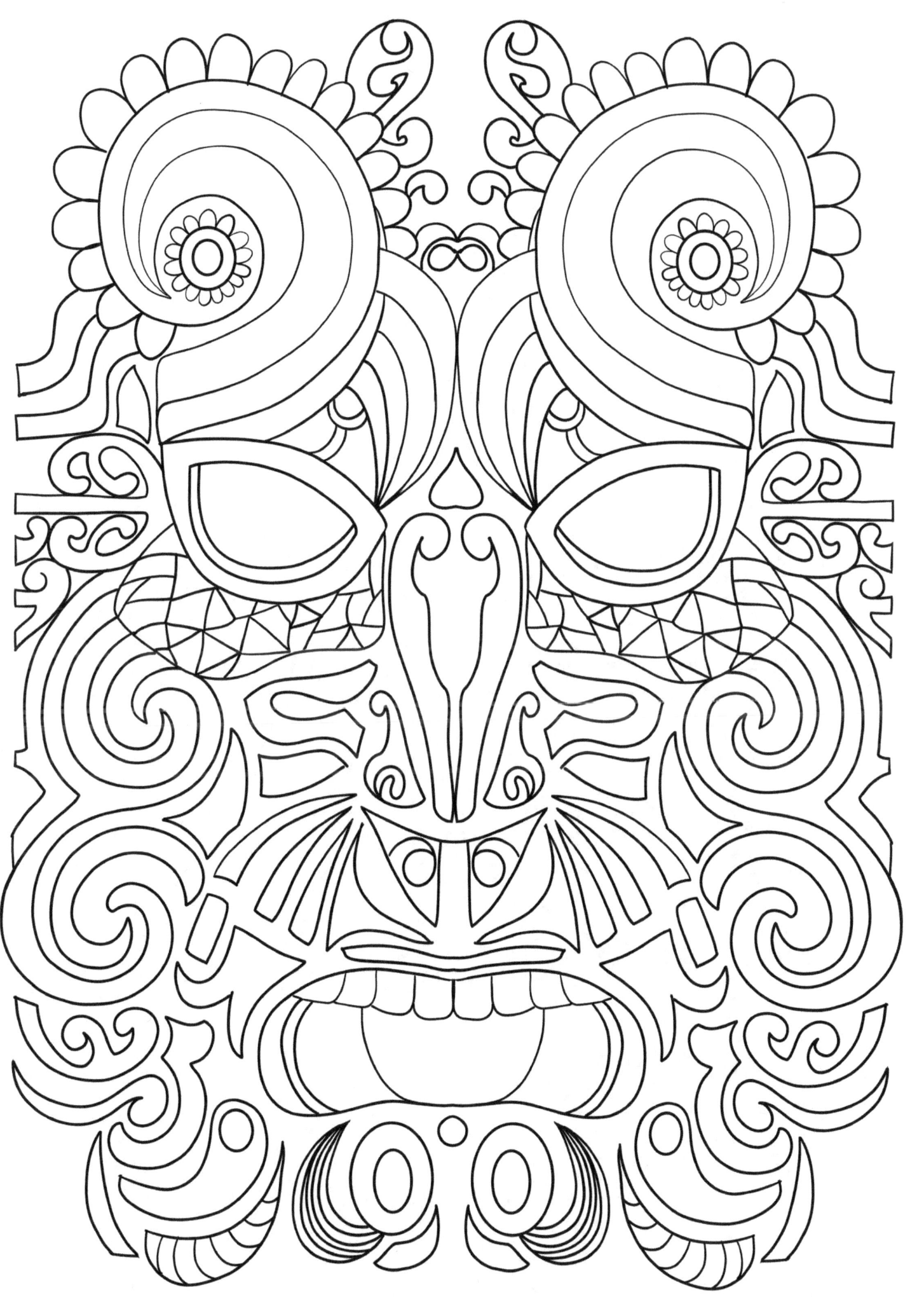

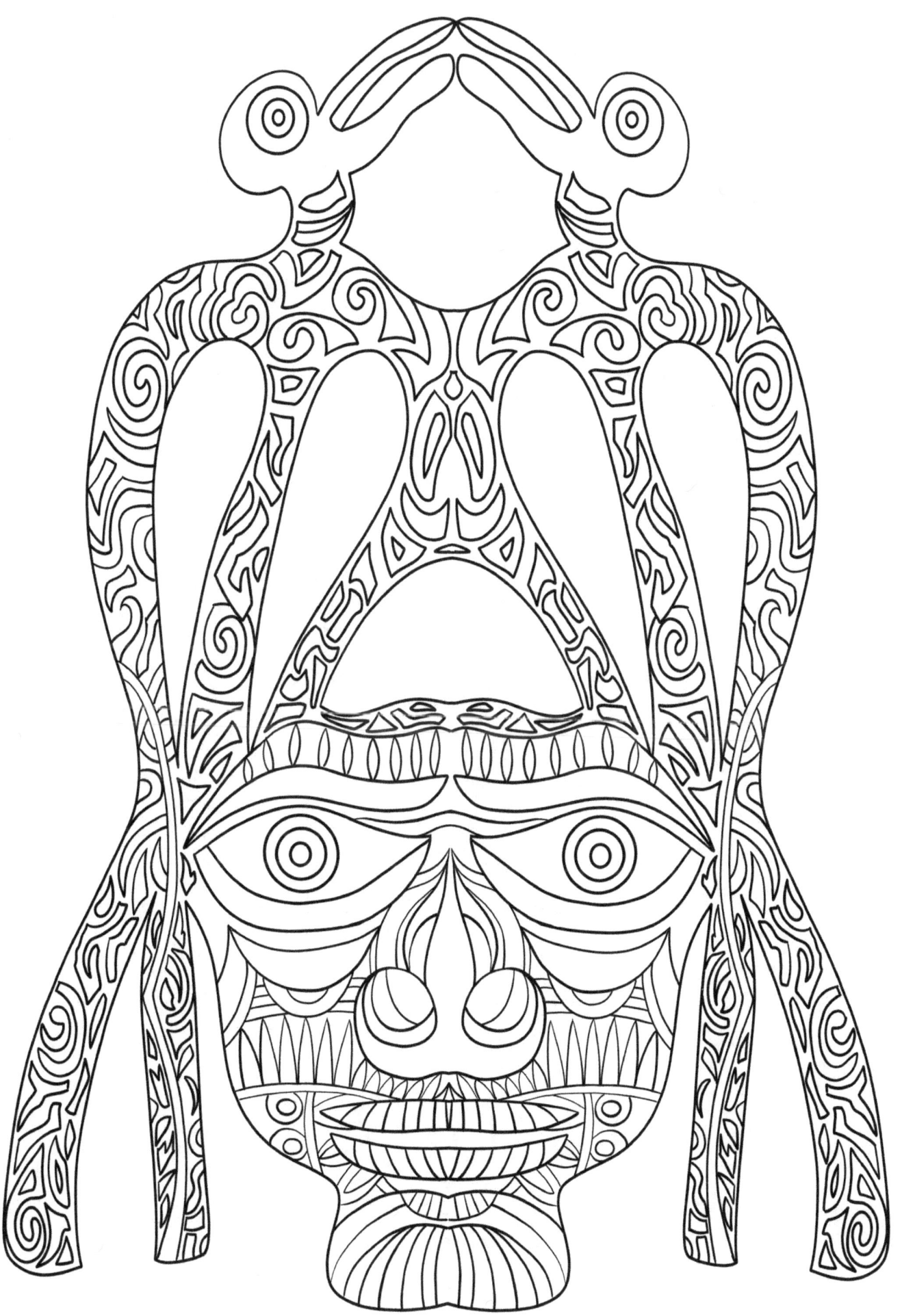

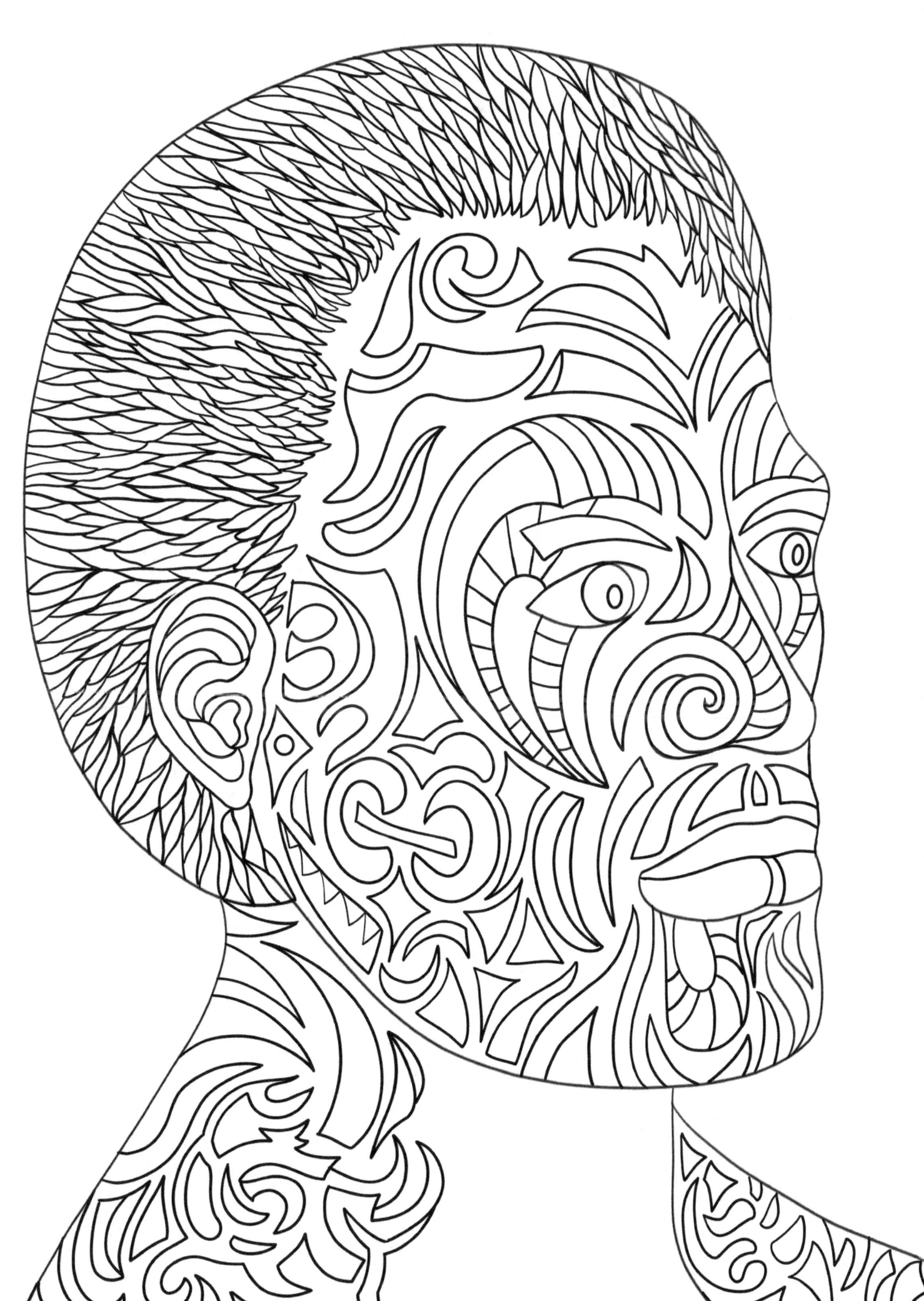

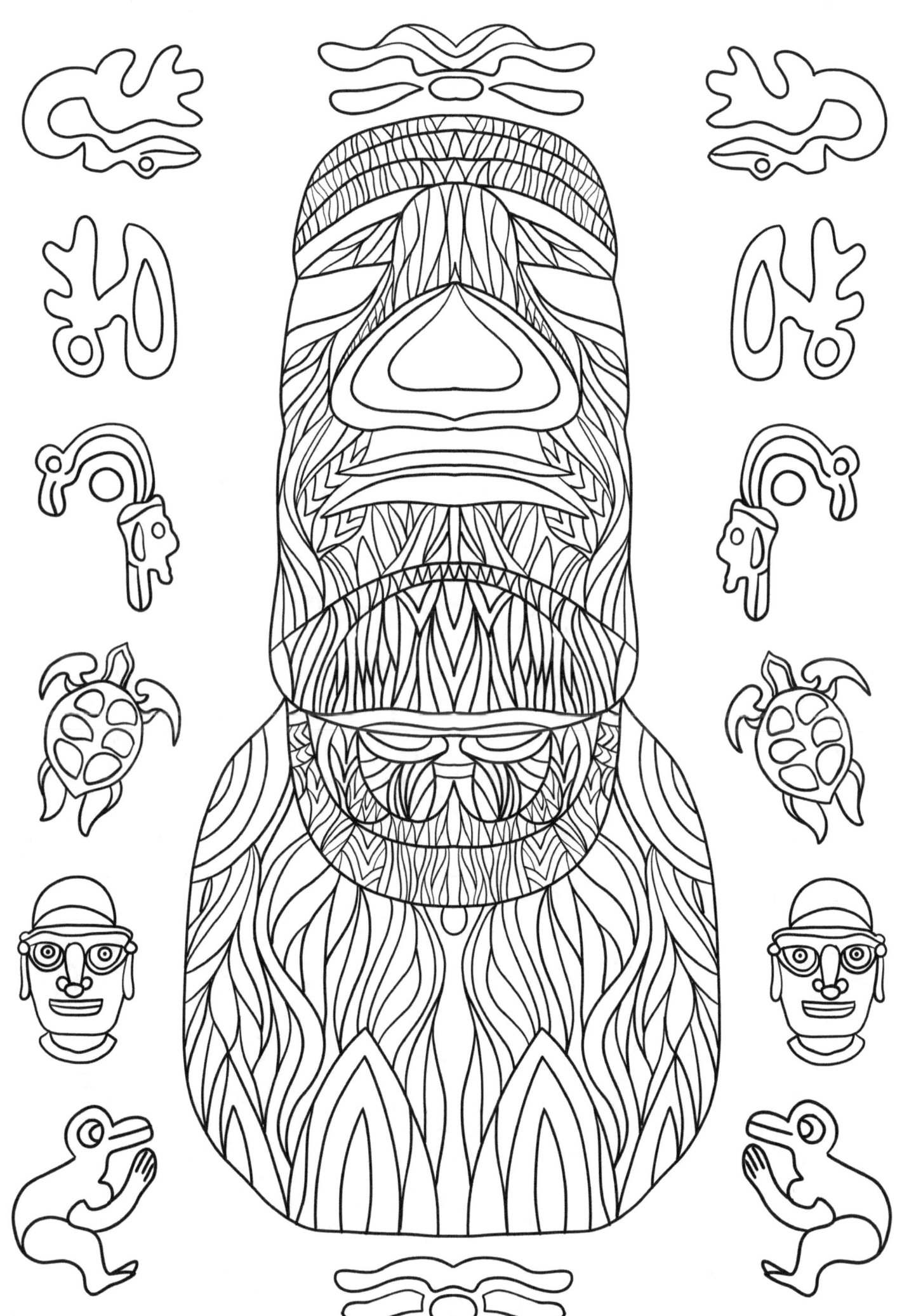

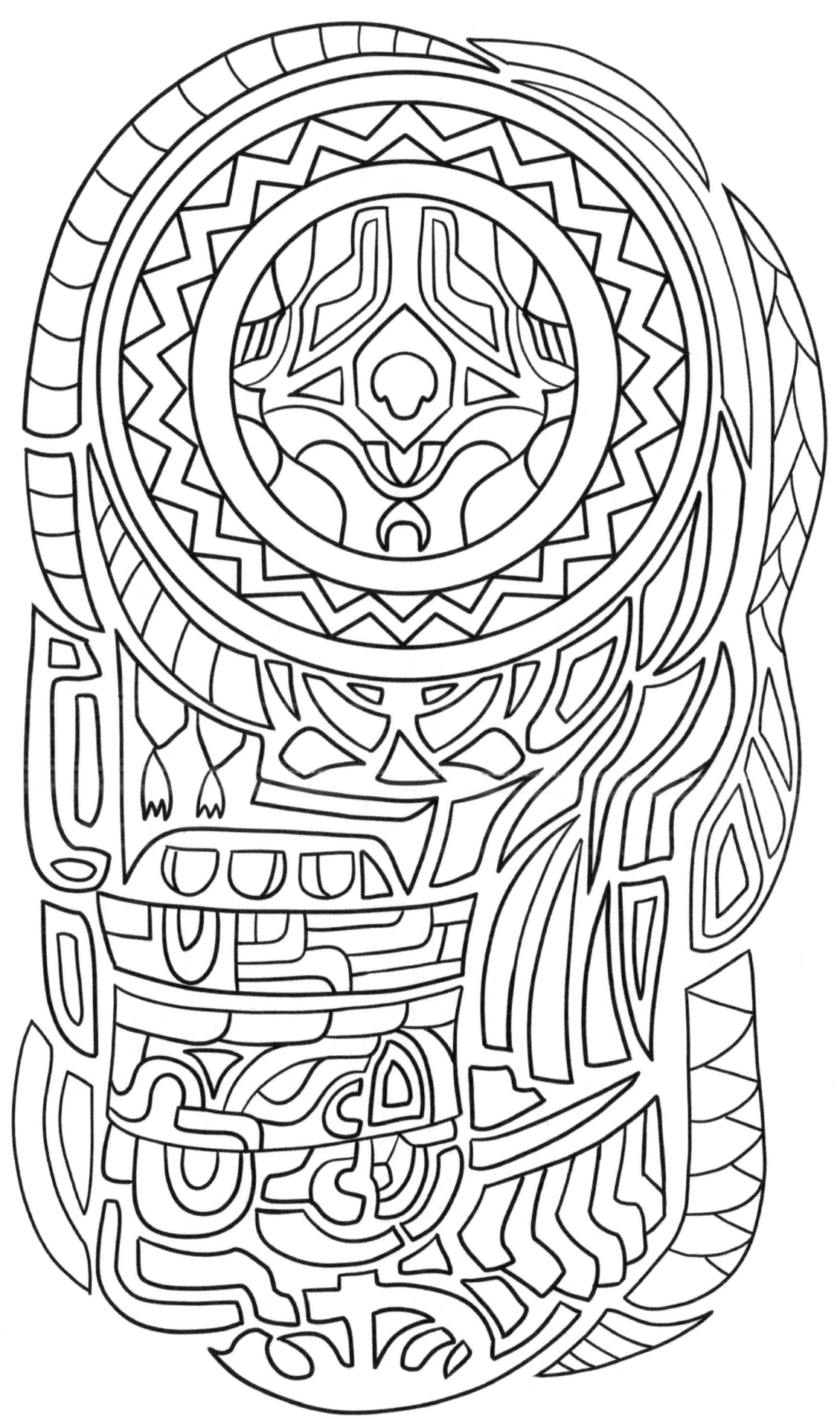

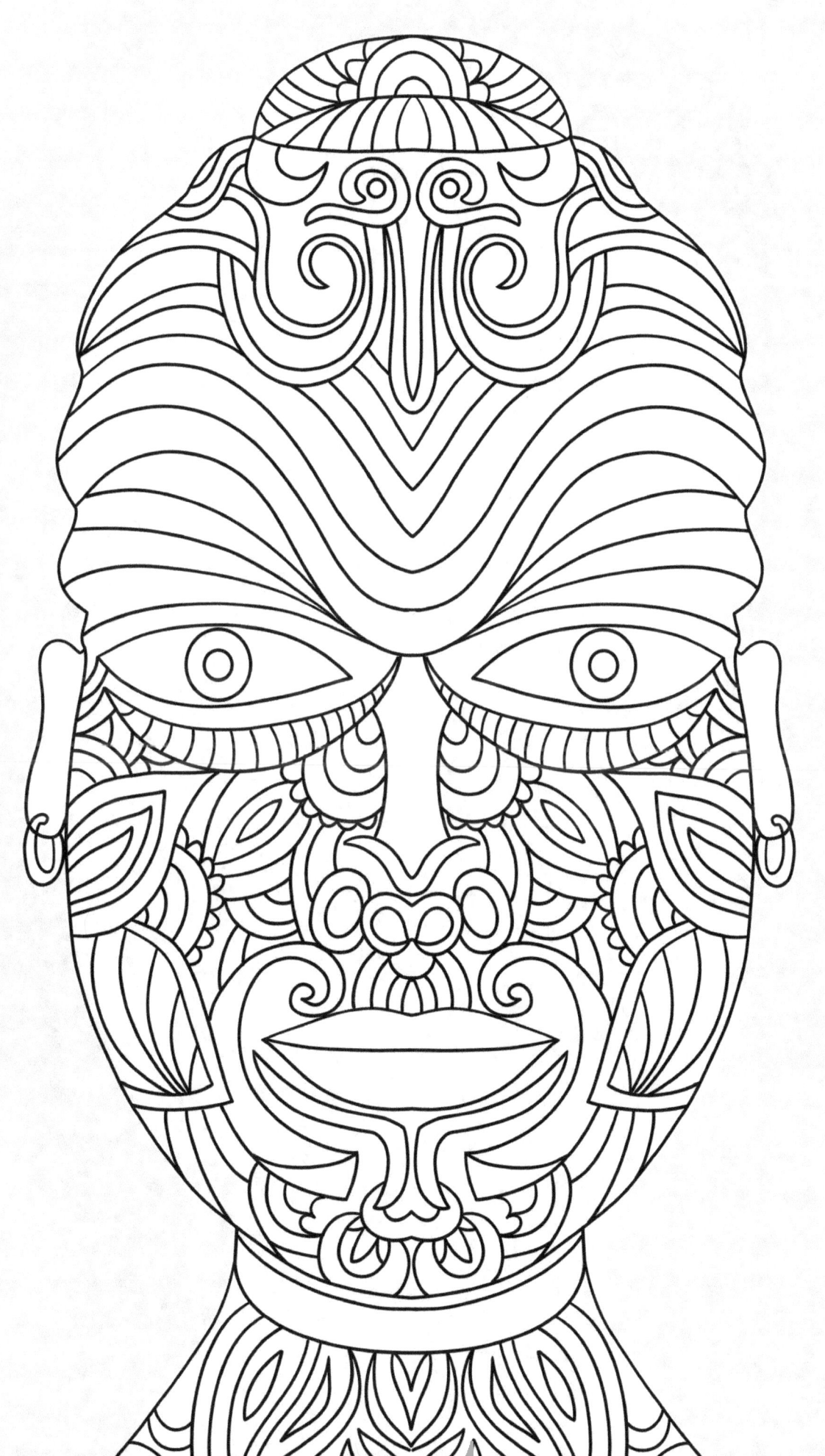

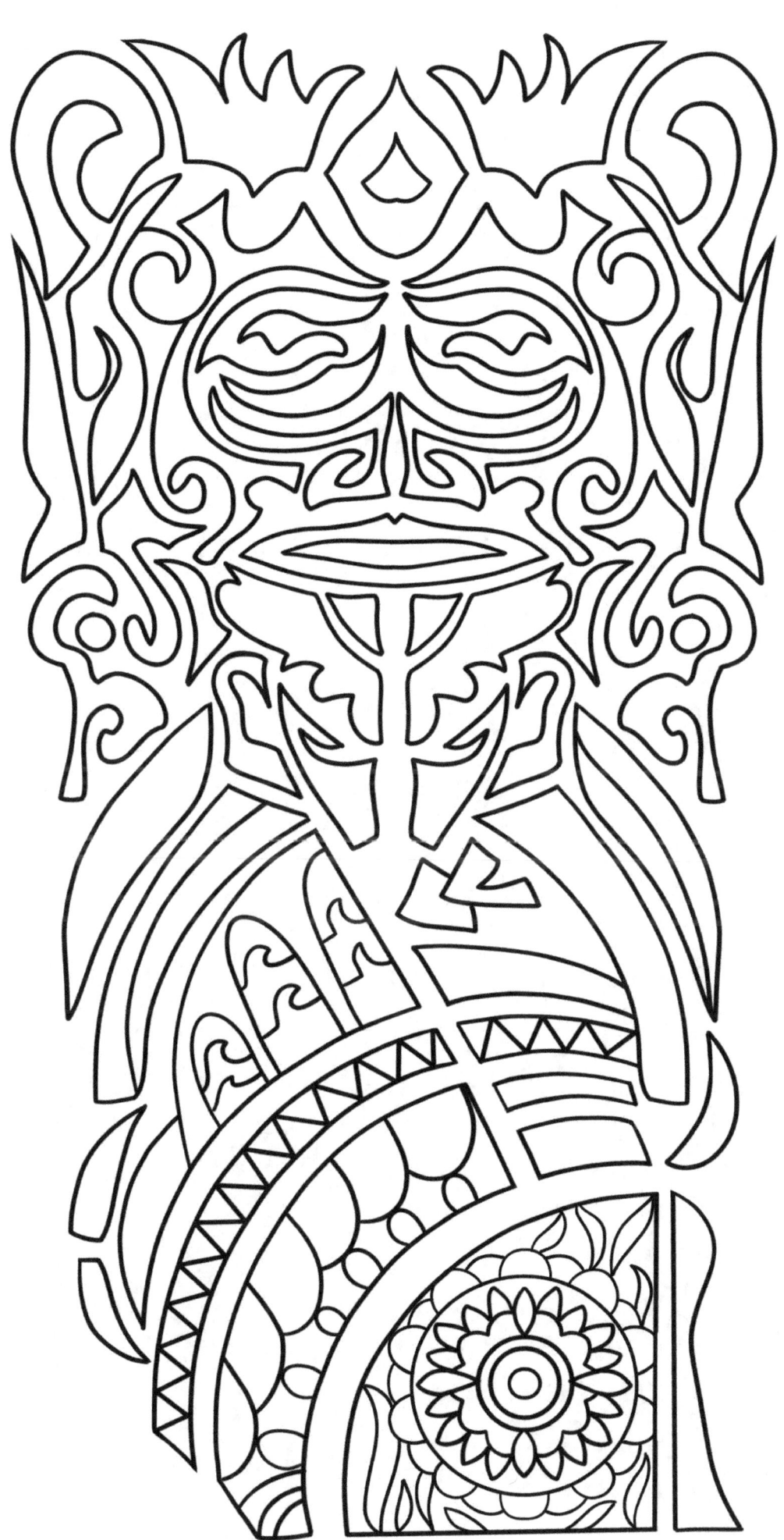

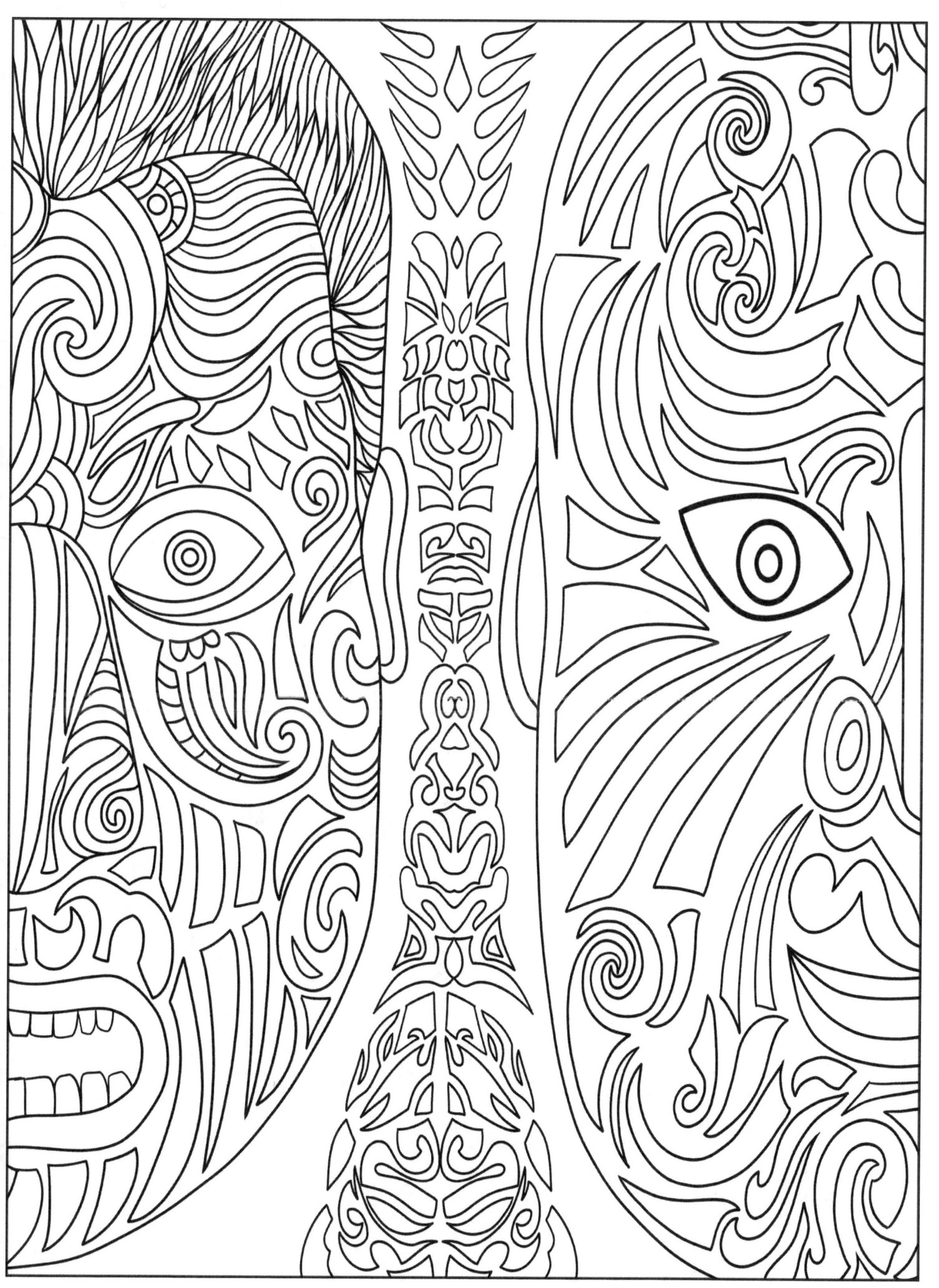

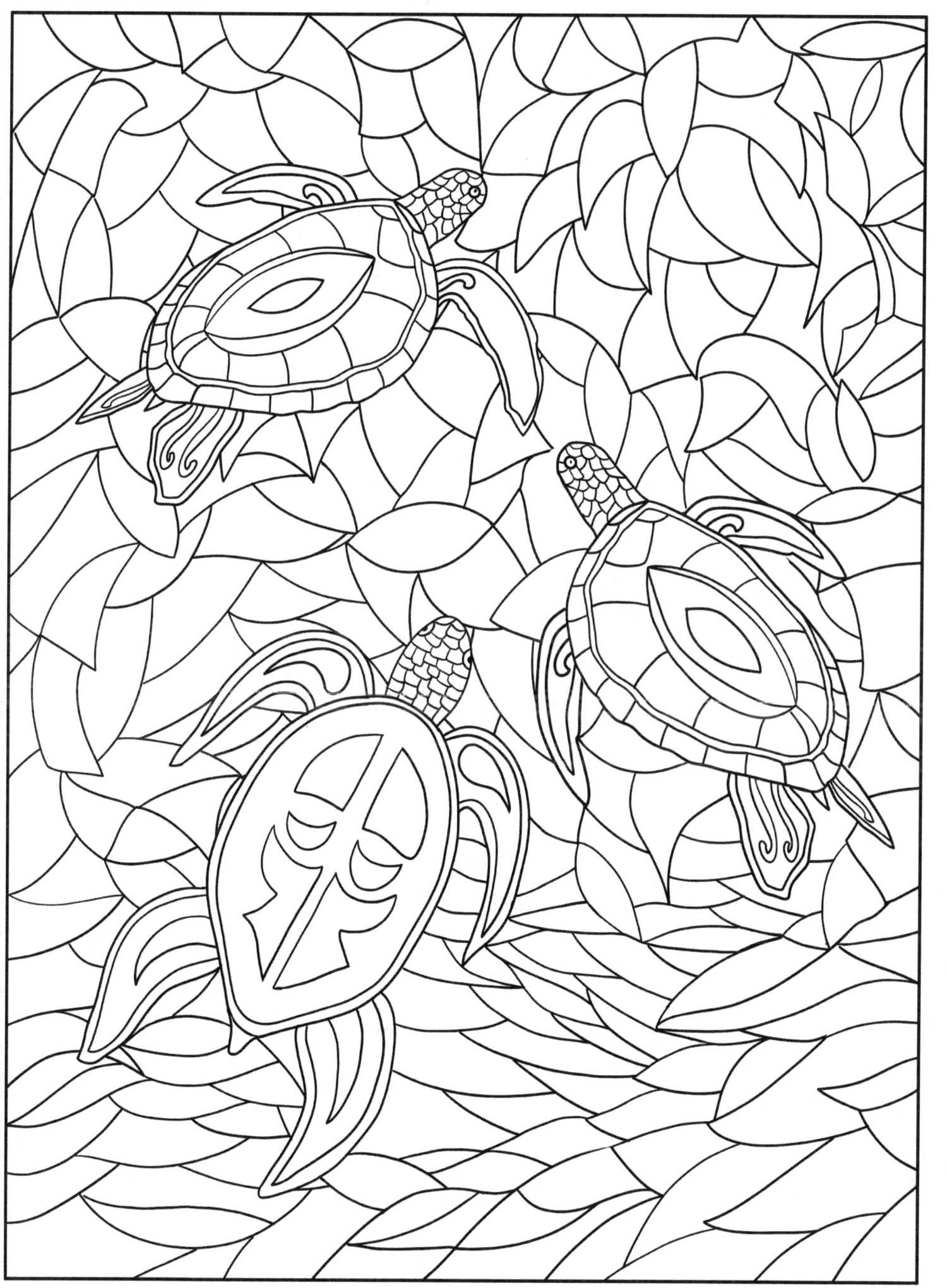

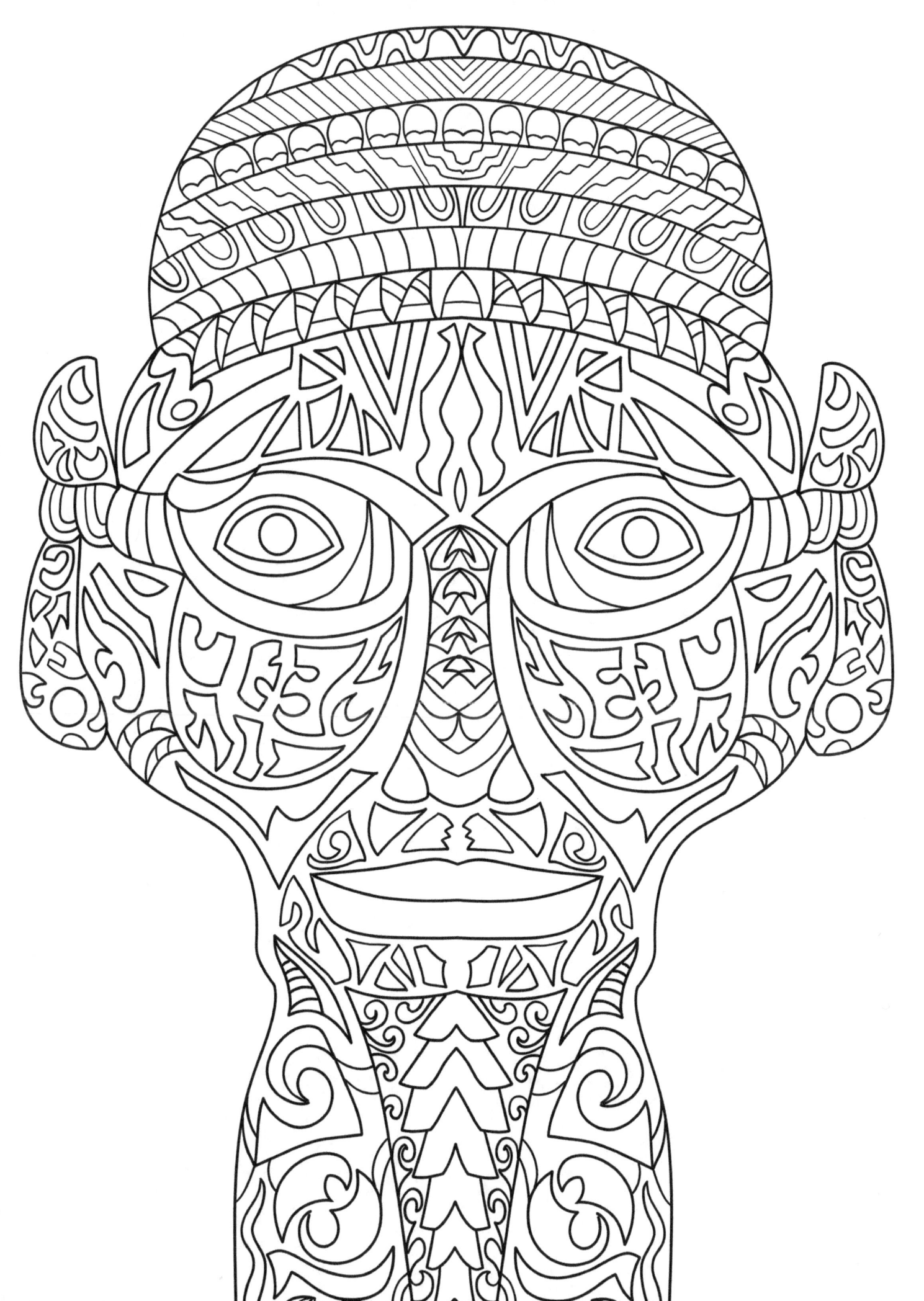

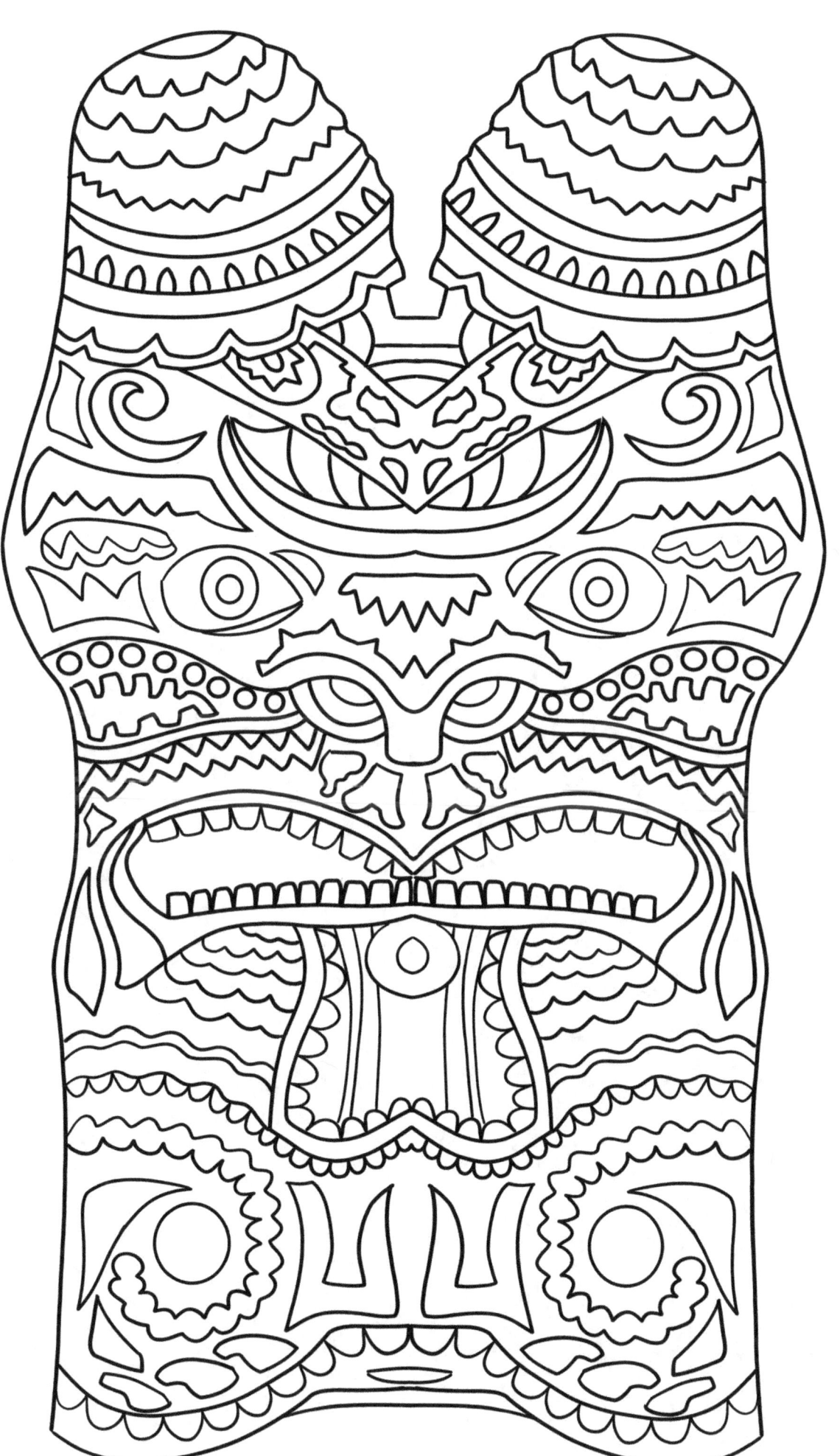

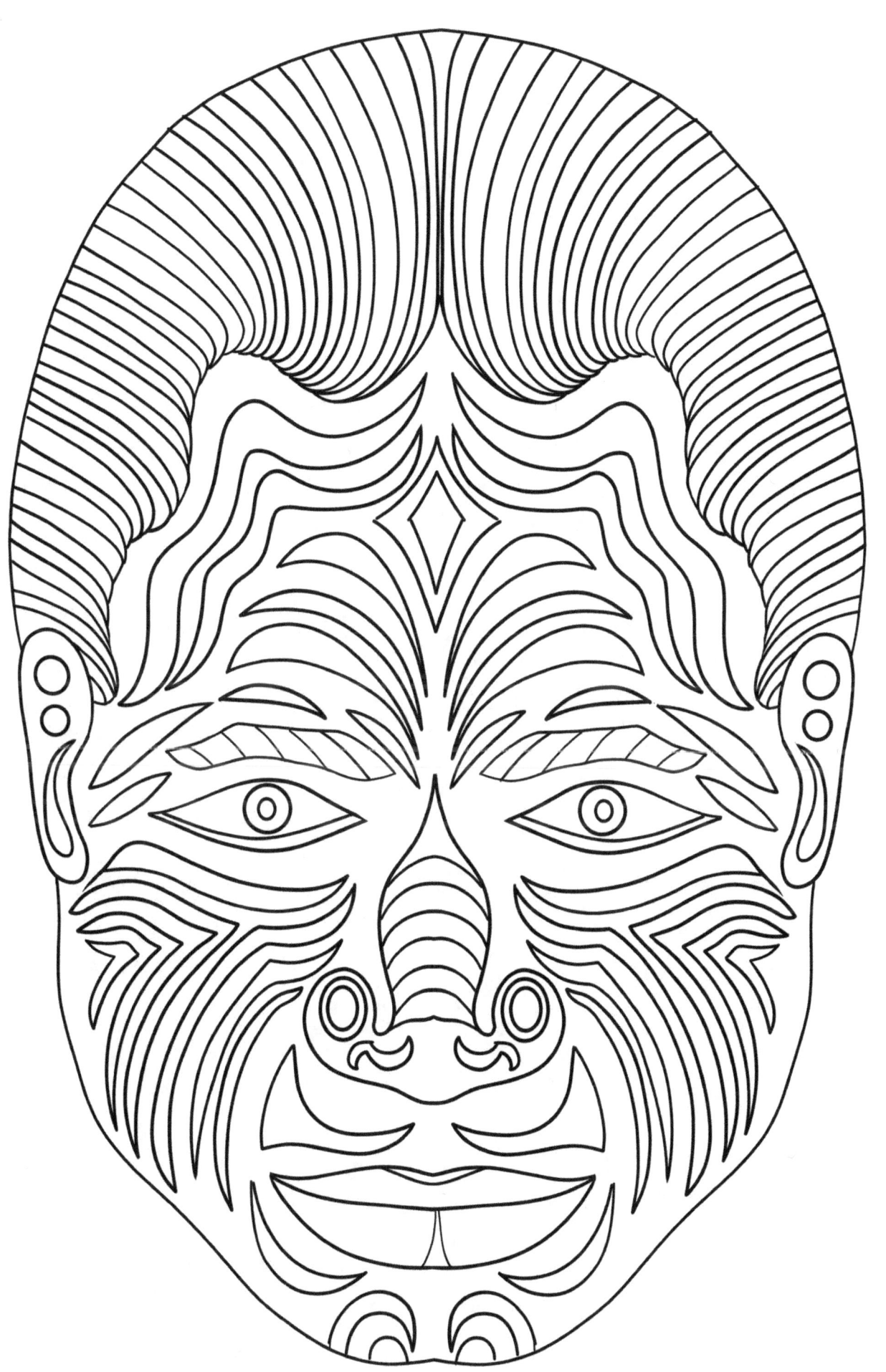

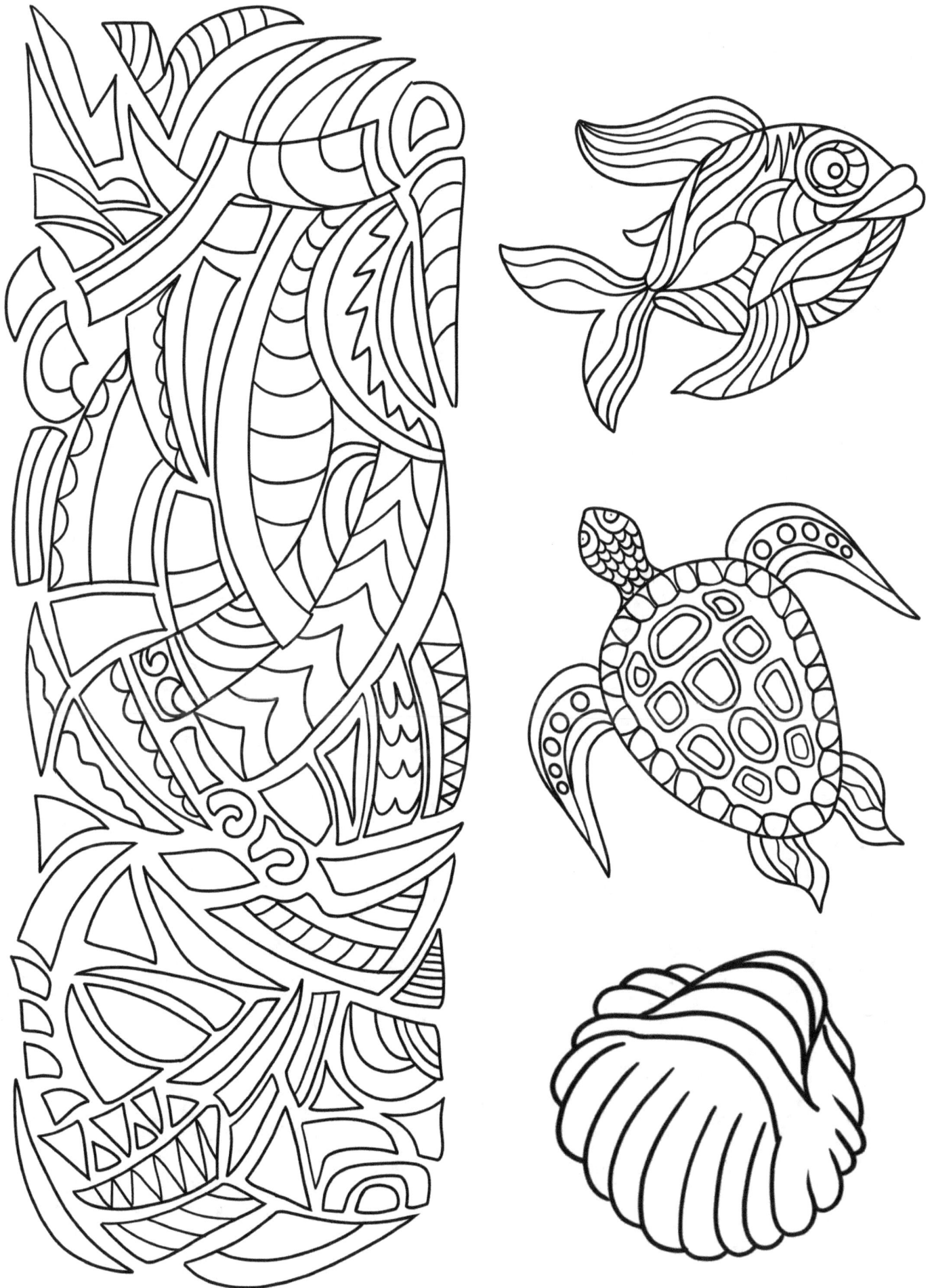

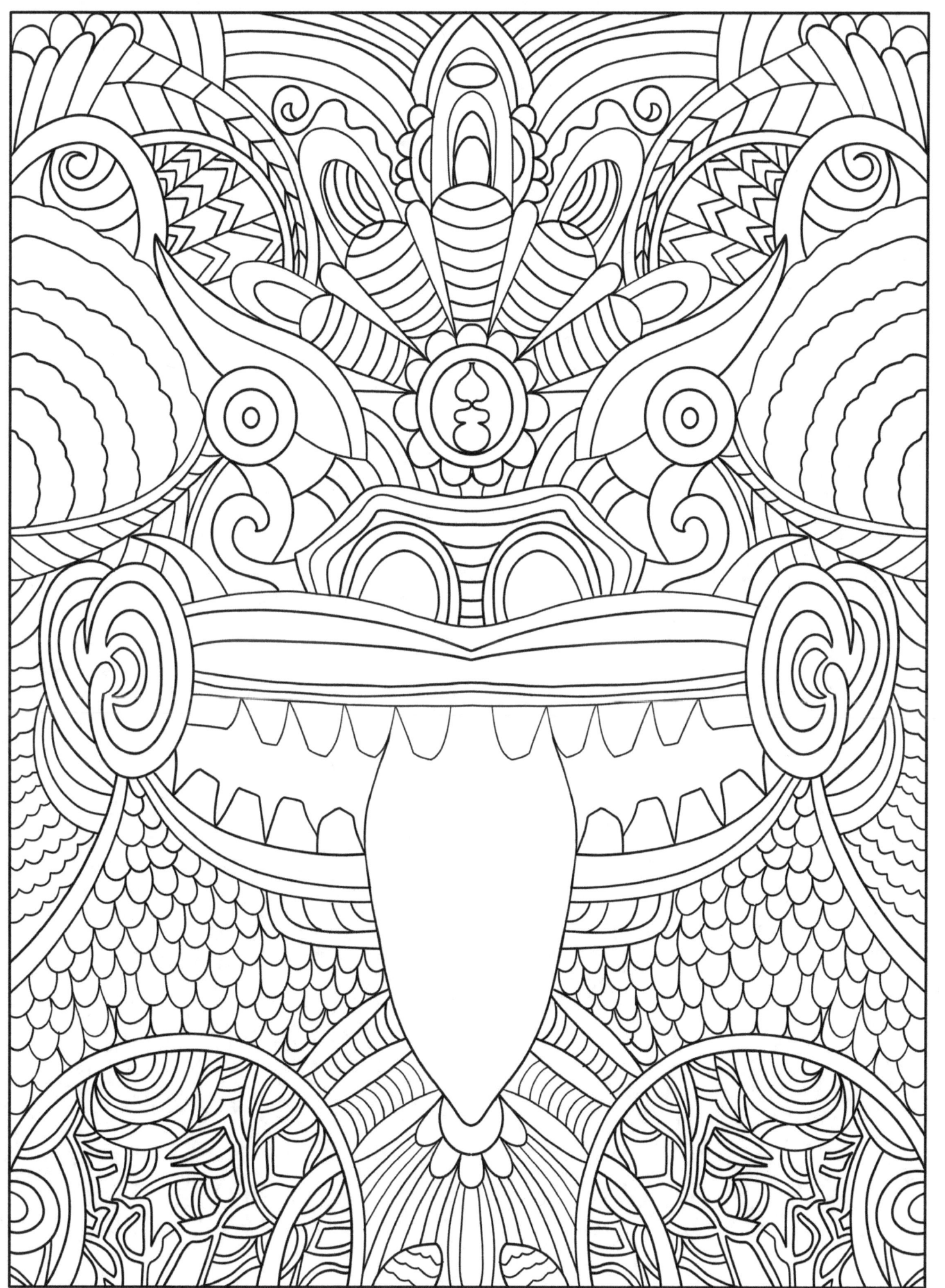

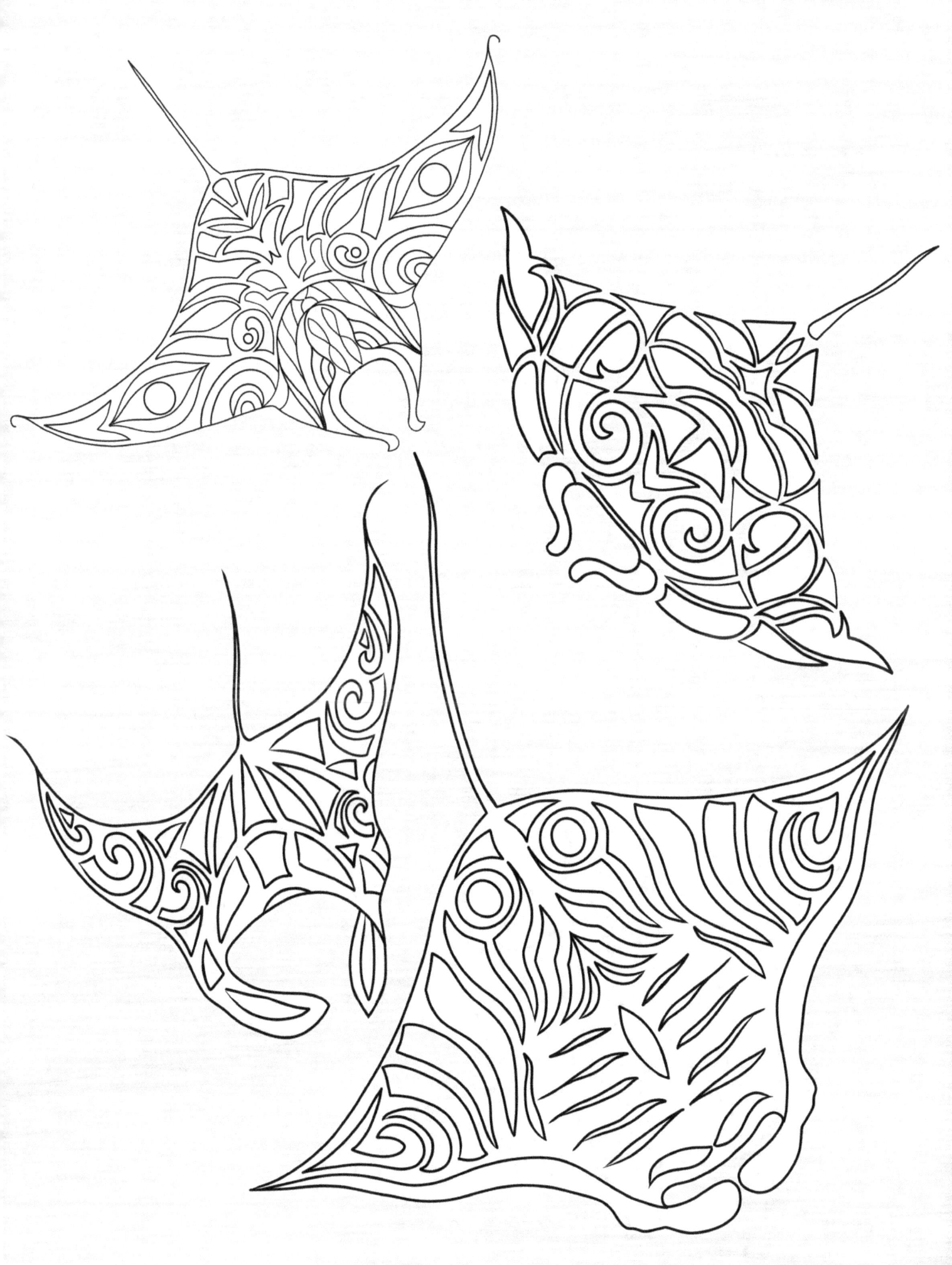

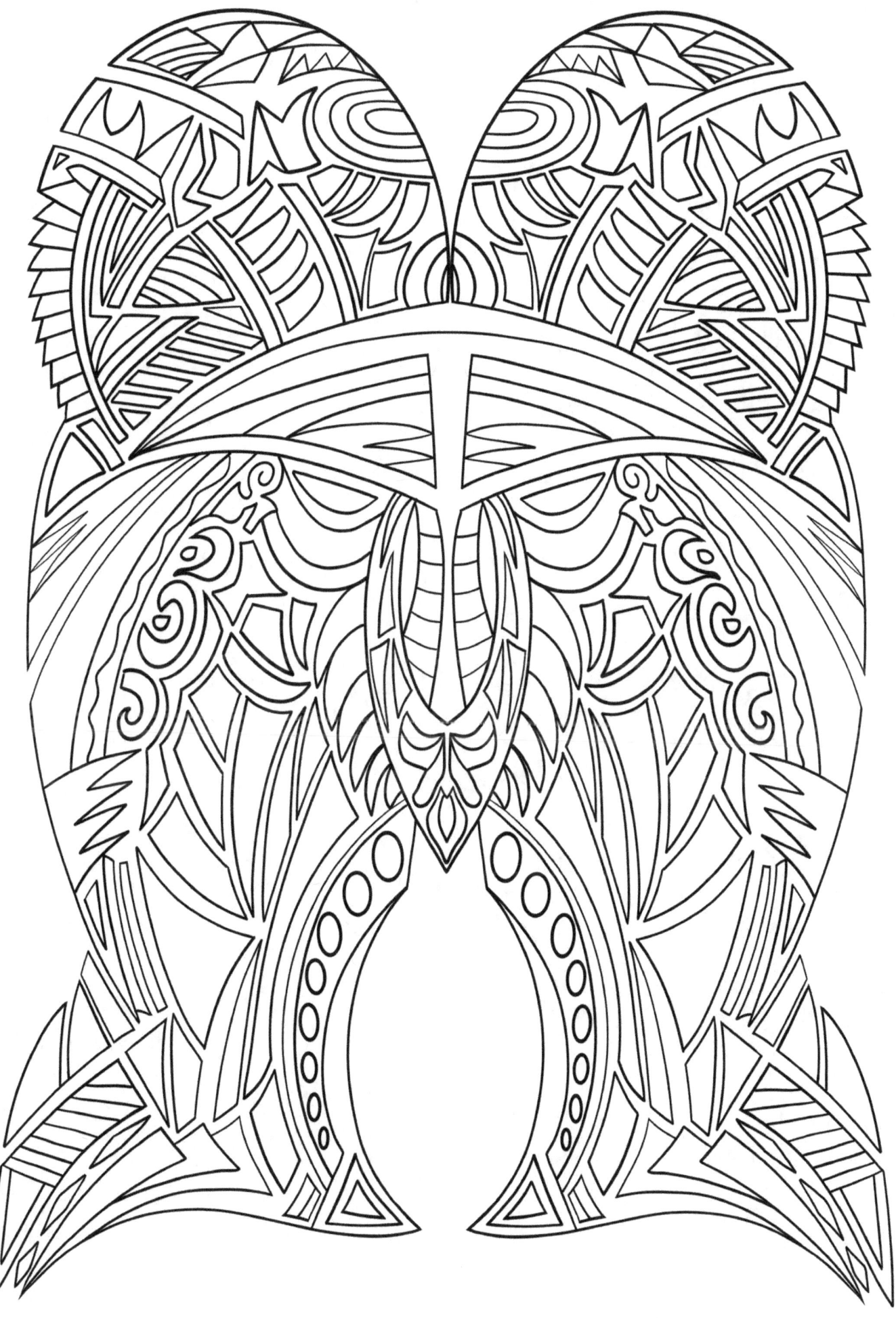

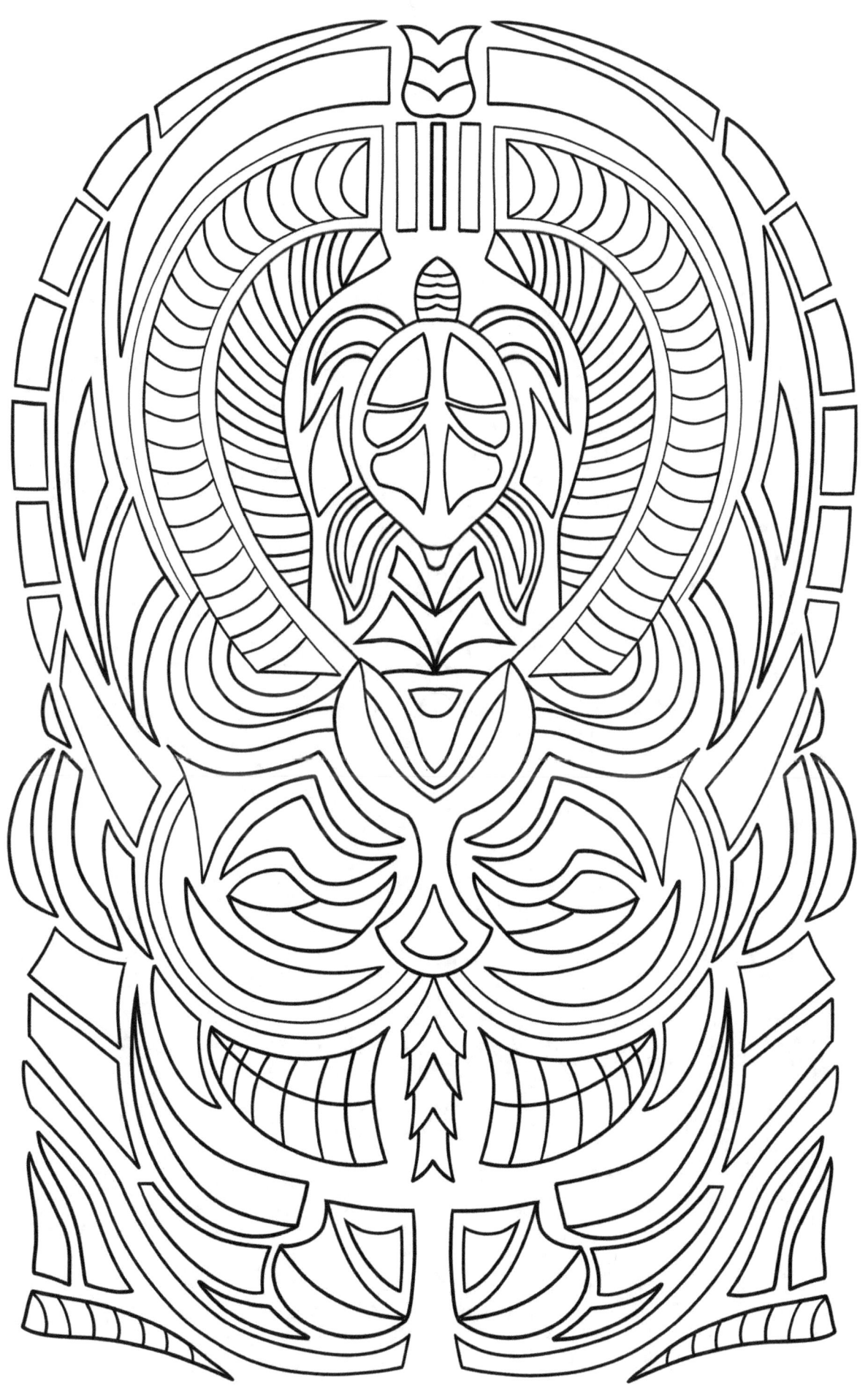

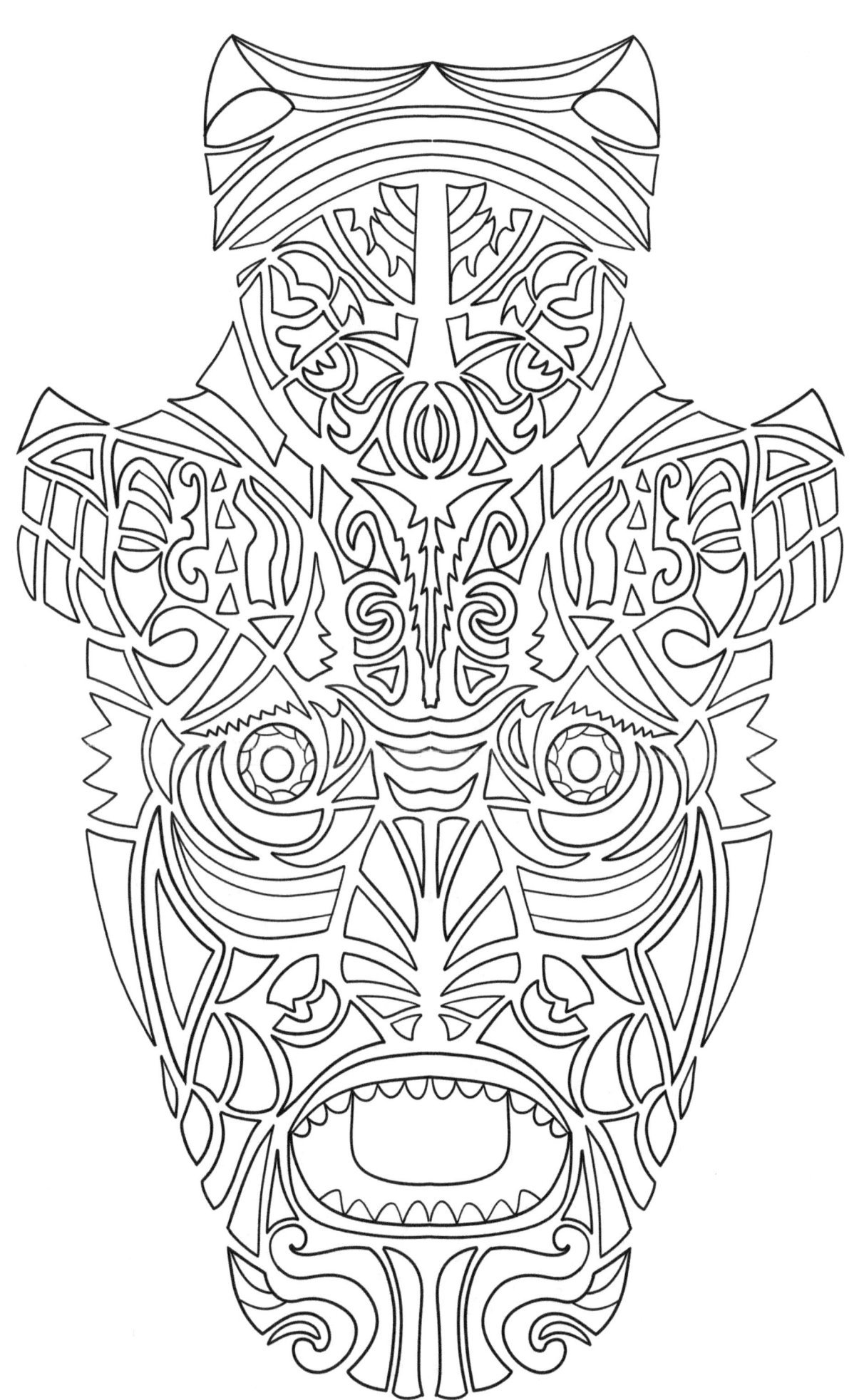

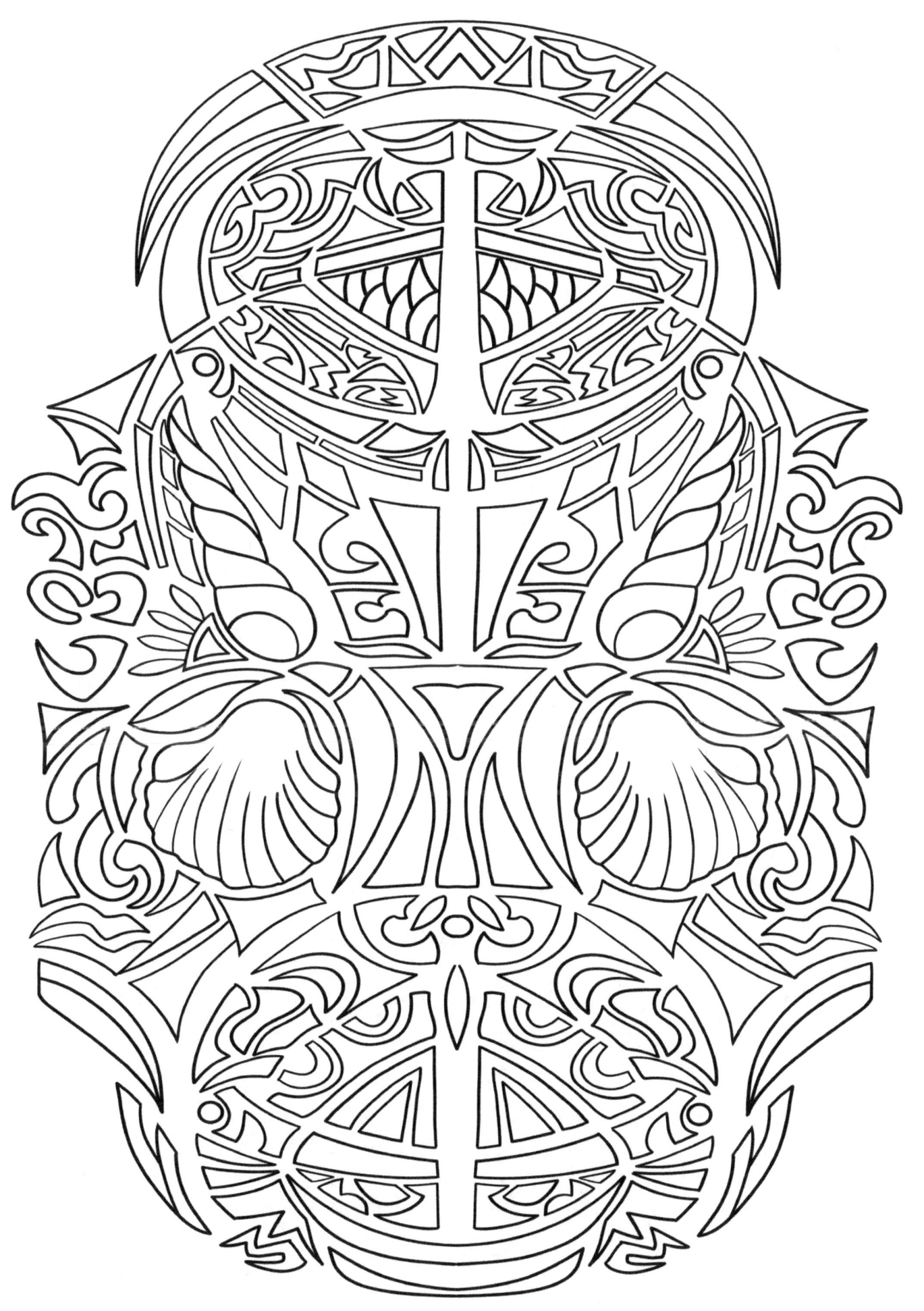

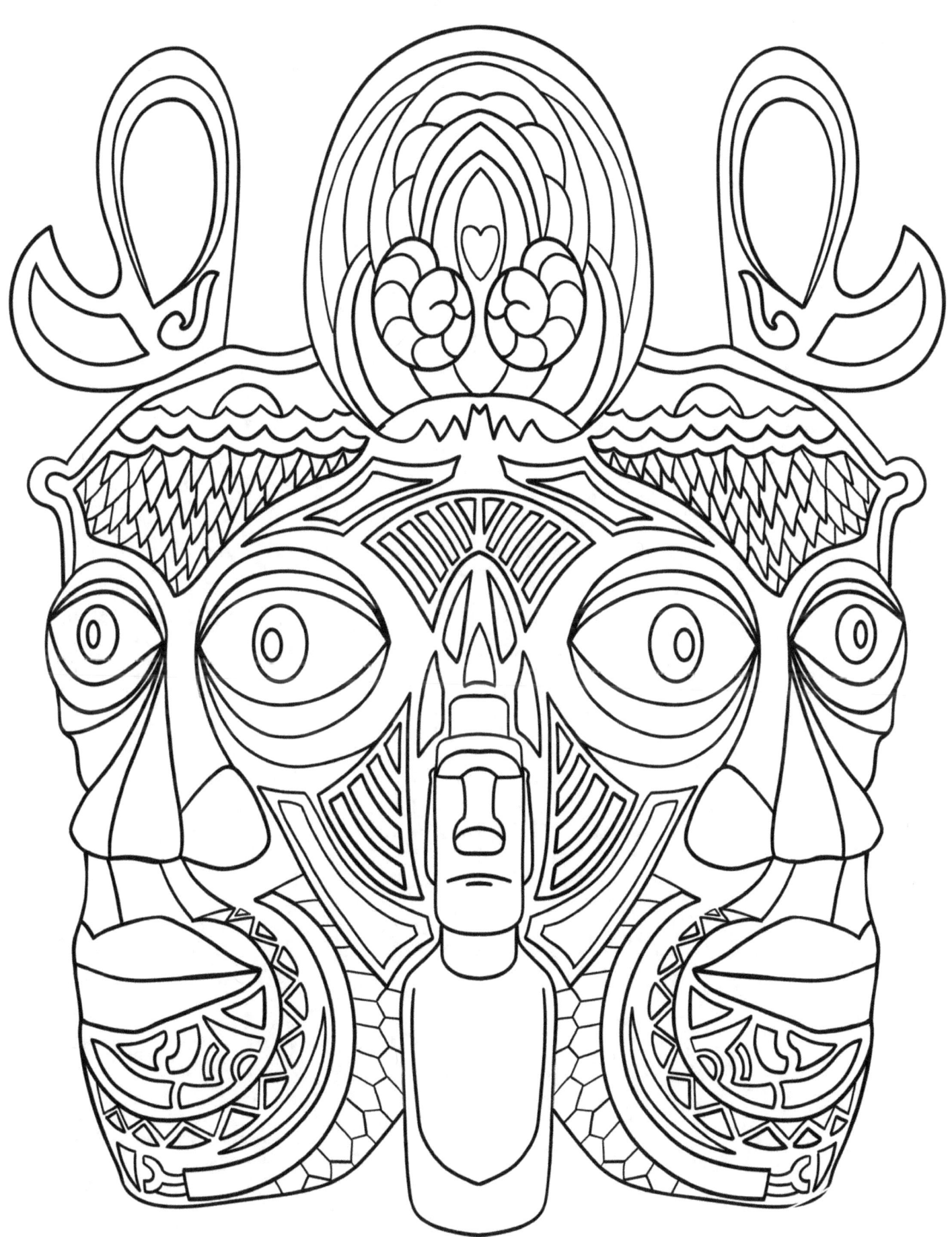

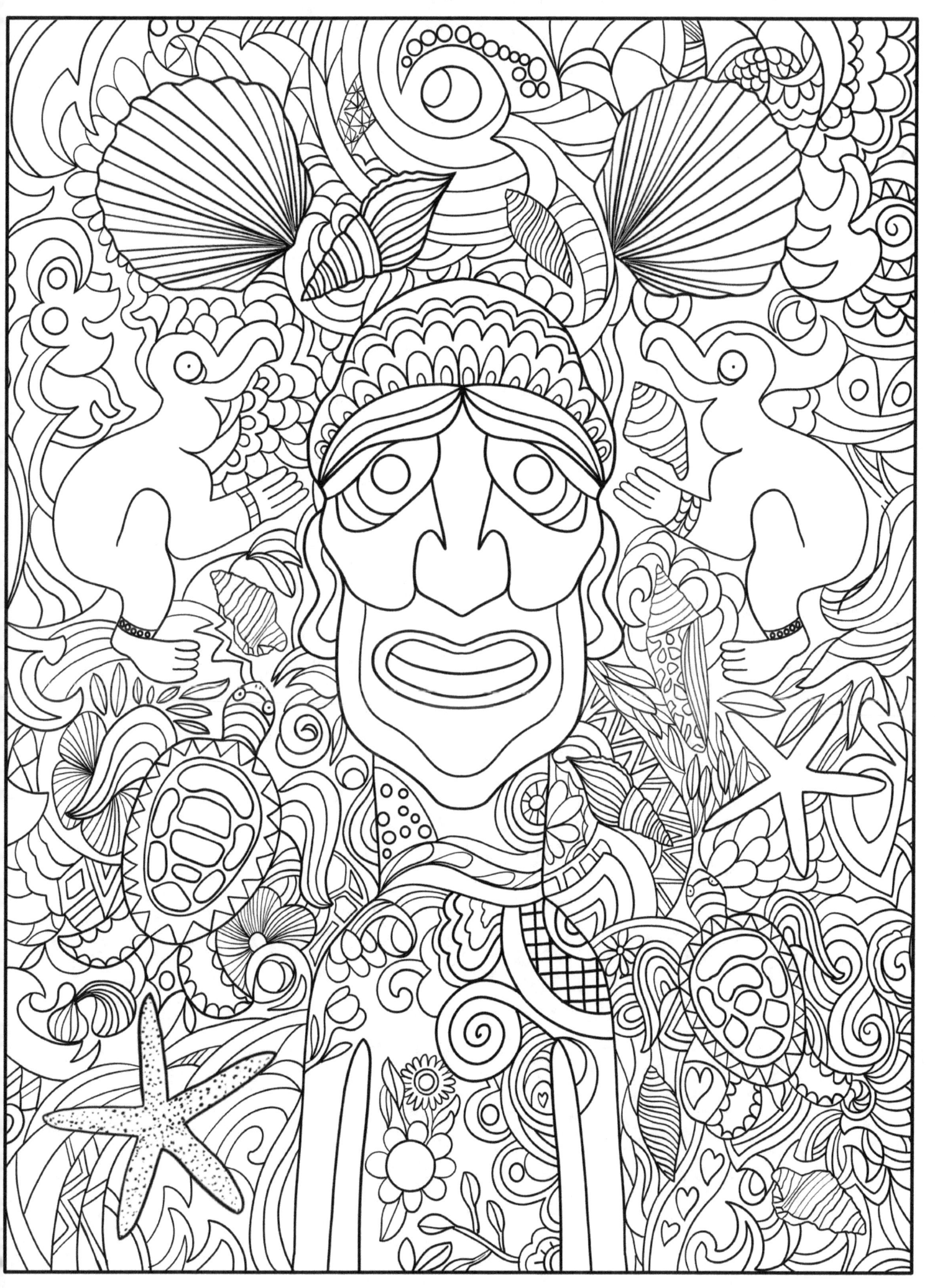

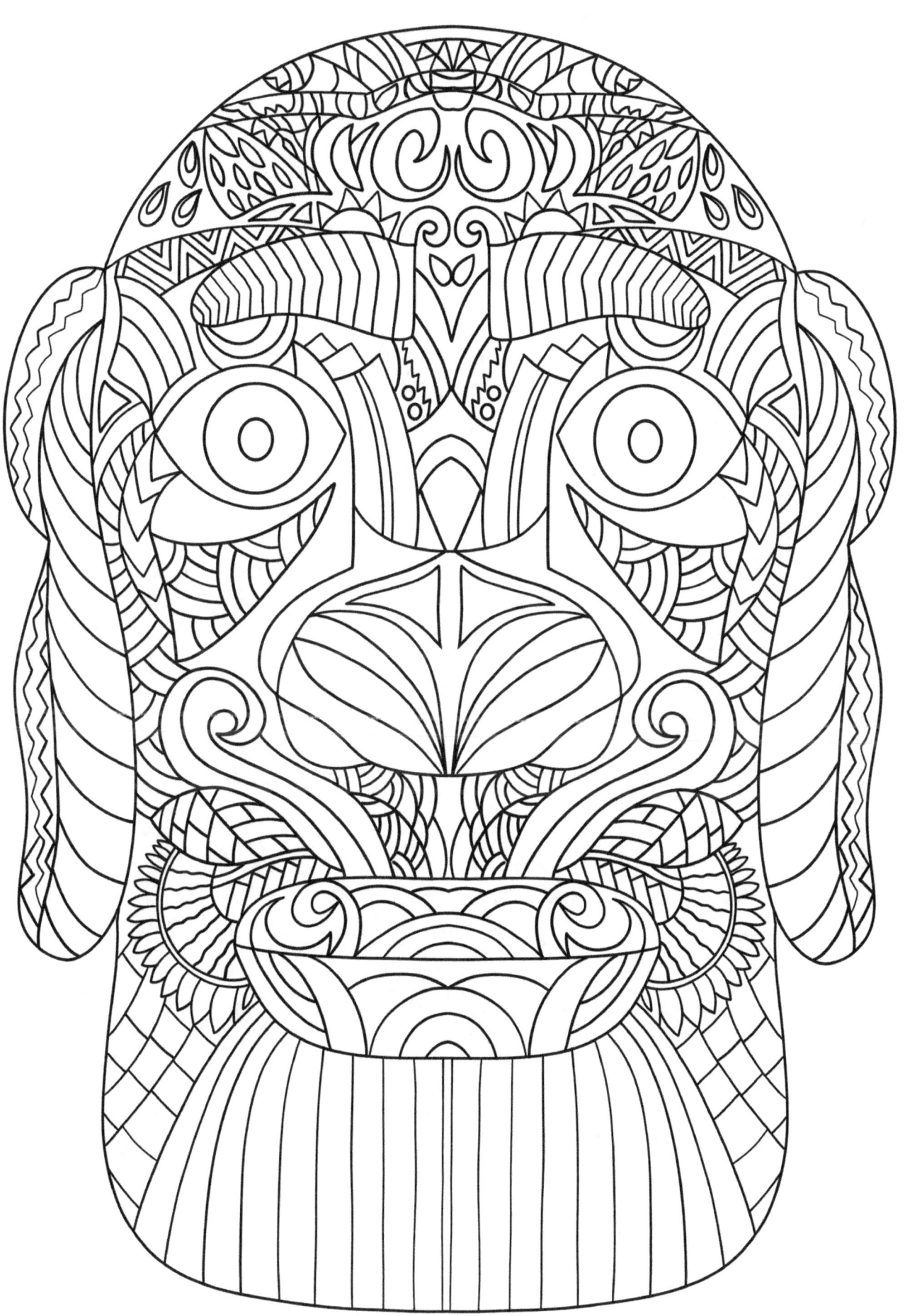

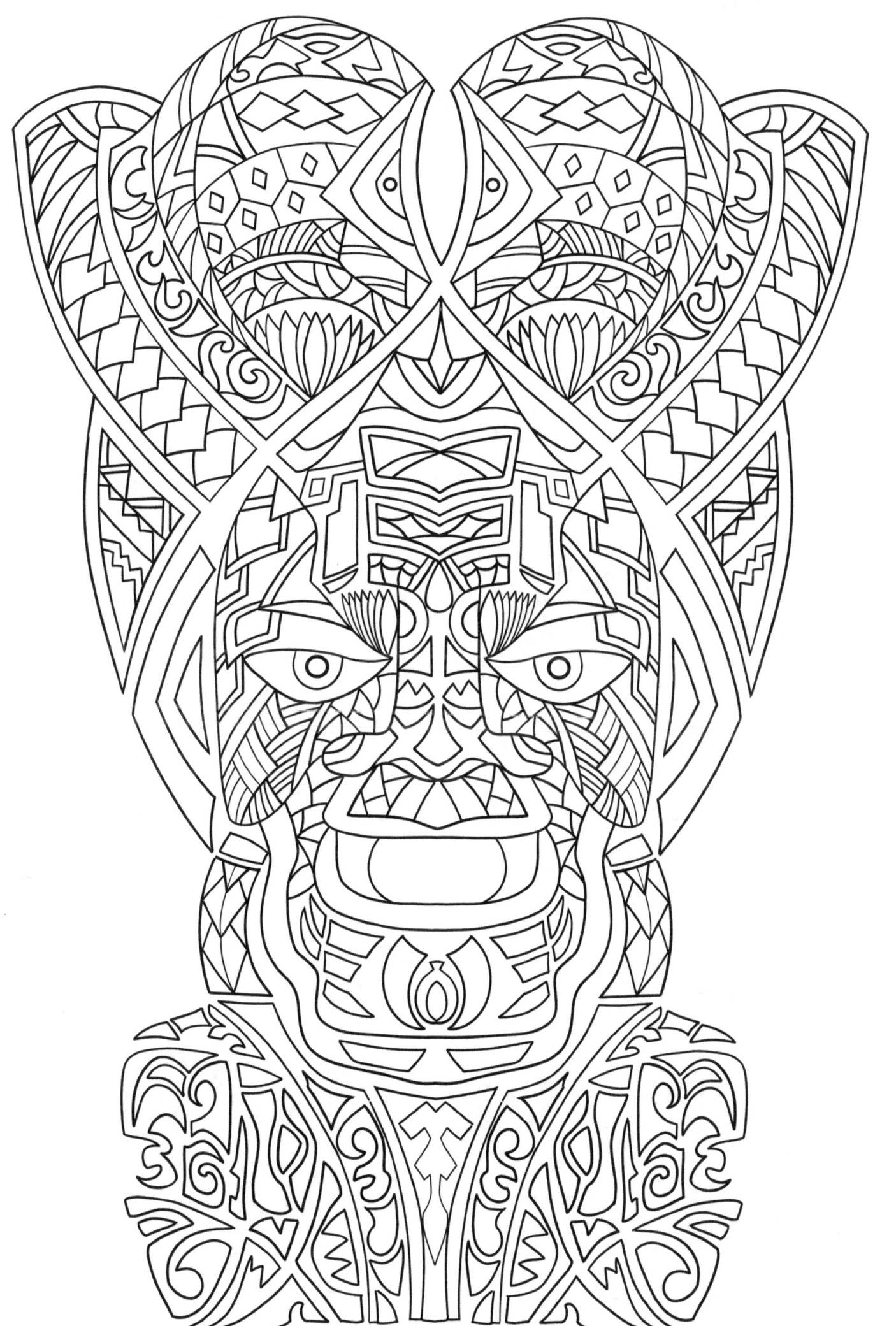

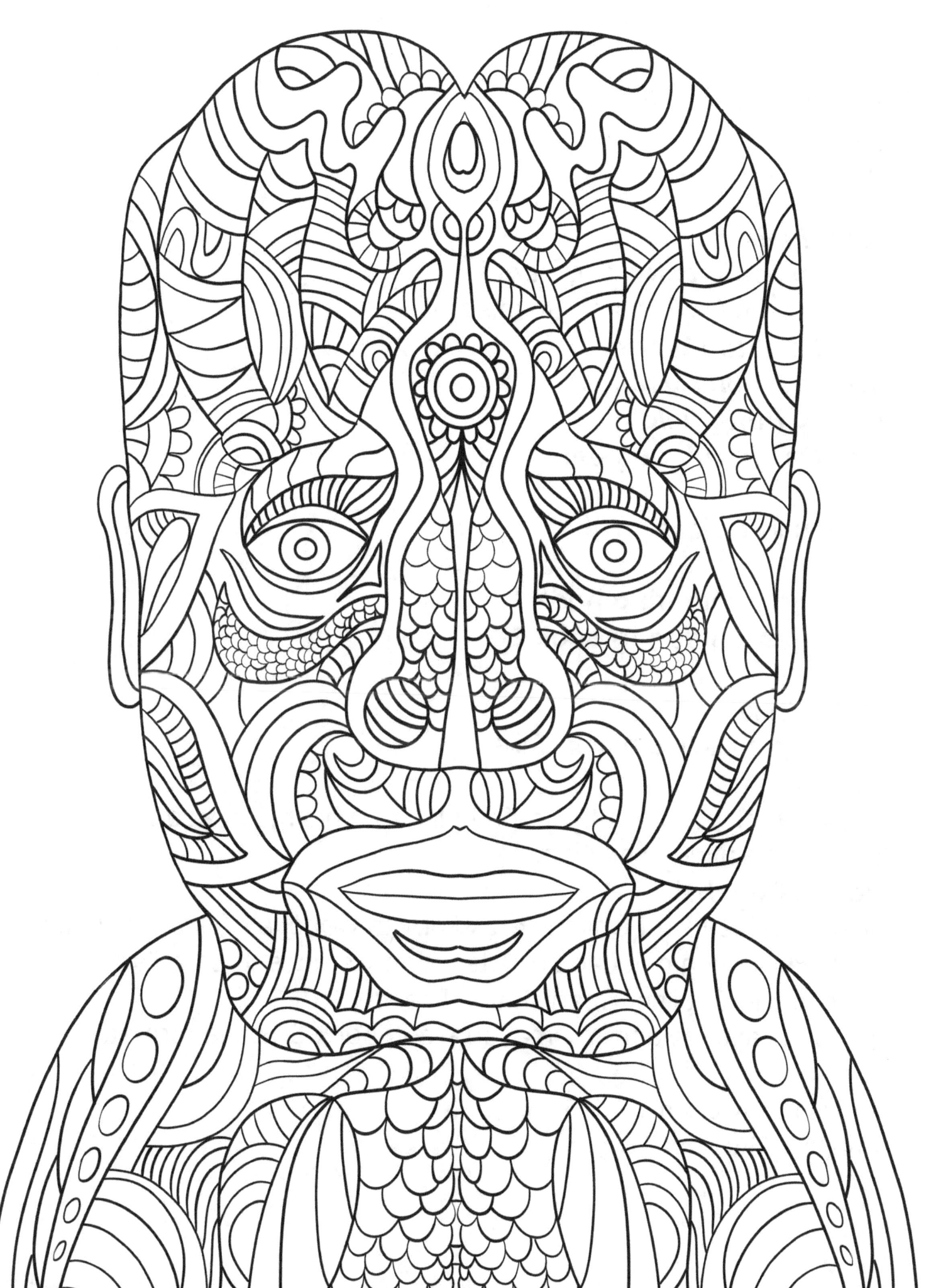

Also by Jorge Lulić

Children's books:

'Mr Armadillo'
'Mr Armadillo colouring book'
(Available in English and Spanish)
'The Lambton Worm'
'The Blaydon Races'
'Cushy Butterfield'
'The Bamburgh Serpent'

Other publications:

'Alebrijes' colouring book 1
'Alebrijes' colouring book 2

'Dear Chile'
A photographic journal of Chile
'Reunion'
Depicting oil paintings by Jorge Lulić from his most recent Spanish painting exhibition.
'Jovita Concha'
Based on the life of Chilean artitst Jovita Concha - A life dedicated to art - Una vida dedicada al Arte - Une vie consacrée à l'art – Available in English, Spanish and French.
All books available from Amazon – soft back & kindle format.

www.jorgelulic.com
jorgelulic556@gmail.com

www.ingramcontent.com/pod-product-compliance
Lightning Source LLC
Chambersburg PA
CBHW062226220526
45471CB00009B/3361